Karl König

Karl König: My Task

Autobiography and Biographies

Karl König

Edited by Peter Selg

Floris Books

Karl König Archive, Vol 1
Subject: Karl König's Biography

Translated by Irene Czech and Regina Erich

Peter Selg's biography of Karl König, revised for this publication
was first published in German in 2000 as part of
Anfänge anthroposophischer Heilkunst by Verlag am Goetheanum

This book first published in English by Floris Books in 2008

British Library CIP Data available

ISBN 978-086315-628-1

Printed in Great Britain
by Athenaeum Press, Gateshead

Contents

Foreword 7

Autobiographical Fragment *Karl König* 11

A Biographical Sketch *Peter Selg* 55

Life with Dr König *Anke Weihs* 131

Some Personal Memories *Hans-Heinrich Engel* 149

Appendix 159

Notes 165

Bibliography 169

Index 171

Foreword

Over the course of the years Karl König (1902–66), the founder of the worldwide Camphill movement, repeatedly reviewed his life story. He wanted to see how the course of his life would unfold under the difficult conditions of the twentieth century. In his thirty-seventh year, he had to flee from his Central European home, threatened by the Nazis because of his Jewish origin and his anthroposophical views and activities. As for many others, losing his home and facing exile was a grave experience for Dr König. Nevertheless he succeeded in establishing his life's work in a foreign country, placing the treatment and care of the child with special needs at the centre of his endeavours.

In darkness living ...
Create an inner sun!
In substance weaving
The spirit's joy is won
(Rudolf Steiner)[1]

Even during his lifetime, many people enquired about the background and the inner motives in König's enigmatic life. Who was this short man who seemed to come from a different era of time, who was gifted with genius and whose work arose out of a far-reaching morality and conscience — in ways which radiated effectiveness and seemed to make the impossible possible? During the last year of his life, König began to write a detailed lyrical and factual description of his life, aware of the many questions directed to him. He touched, with greatest modesty, on the meaningful points of his life, towards the founding of Camphill. An attempt to write an autobiographical description was soon abandoned. König only got as far as the successful flight to London, or rather, to the receipt of permission to enter Great Britain. This 'Autobiographical Fragment' was published three years after his death in a journal in several instalments. Eventually in 1979 it was made available as a small book by the Circle of Friends of Camphill with a preface by Carlo Pietzner. Thirteen years later the first comprehensive biography appeared in Germany in 1992, a detailed description of Karl König's vita, researched for several years and written by König's medical student and colleague Hans Müller-Wiedemann. Based on this profound study, Karl König's autobiographical notes and numerous other sources Peter Selg wrote a detailed introduction to König's life and works which was published in Switzerland as part of a collected edition on the founders of anthroposophical medicine at the beginning of the twenty-first century.[2]

The volume presented here is part of Karl König's collected works and offers an introduction to Karl König's personal and professional course of life. It combines Karl König's autobiographical fragment and Peter Selg's essay, as well as two selected reminiscences written by his colleagues Anke Weihs and Hans-Heinrich Engel. Anke Weihs (1914–87) was born in Australia and met Dr König in Vienna as his patient. She belonged to the group who founded the Camphill community in 1939/40 and remained to be one of its most supportive members until her death. Hans-Heinrich Engel (1921–78), a medical doctor, came to Camphill in 1951. He became a medical staff member of the community and was Karl König's therapist when König encountered serious health problems in the mid 1950s. Anke Weihs's and Hans-Heinrich Engel's reminiscences stand for those of many others; they let us see Dr König from the viewpoint of people who shared their life with him and who were able to see his special qualities at close quarters, without glorification but with deep respect for what they experienced with and through Karl König.

In the years to come, further studies relating to the life of Karl König will appear within the collected works. This work is being done by the Karl König Archive, Aberdeen in co-operation with the Ita Wegman Institute for Basic Research into Anthroposophy, Arlesheim, Switzerland.

Stefan Geider
Richard Steel
Peter Selg

Karl König Archive, Aberdeen
Ita Wegman Institute, Arlesheim
Aberdeen
May 2008

Autobiographical Fragment

Karl König

Countless human settlements are scattered across the world: large and small, significant and insignificant, powerful and poor. Whether town or metropolis, village or hamlet, each has its own 'face' and is unlike any other — it has its own individuality. Its unique features are shaped by the memories of all the events and activities that have taken place in its houses and streets, gardens and avenues, at its squares and fountains, gates and towers. The breadth and depth of human experience forms and moulds the personality of a place; yet people rarely recognize or understand this individuality consciously. Nevertheless, everyone who has grown up or grown old there carries a part of it within themselves. Such a 'personality of place' expresses itself through the way we speak, the particular melody of our gestures and in the unique colours of our experiences and perceptions. And when arriving in a foreign city to settle and live, it is not easy to harmoniously integrate one's own gestures — already acquired in a previous daily existence — into the new way of life with its quite different rhythms.

It was like that for many of us who were taken away from Vienna and Austria to the north of Scotland — to Aberdeen, which is situated as high up as the northern point of the Jutland

Peninsula and around the same latitude as Gothenburg and Riga. Aberdeen also has its own 'face,' its own individual character. Besides many other things, it is a harbour city; it is also old, and in parts, still emanates a majestic grandeur worthy of regard. Many houses are built out of the grey-silver granite, which is quarried in the immediate area, and no doubt, Aberdeen acquired the name of the 'Silver City' after the colour of this stone. Sky and sea often merge into one another through the mist and rain. Then a grey fog spreads through the streets and a dank dampness seeps into people's homes. The open fireplaces remain lit during both summer and winter so that a little warmth and light is brought into the dark rooms. And sometimes, if I went for a walk through Aberdeen, Theodor Storm's verses would come to mind:

Am grauen Strand, am grauen Meer
Und seitab liegt die Stadt;
Der Nebel drückt die Dächer schwer,
Und durch die Stille braust das Meer
Eintönig um die Stadt.

Upon grey sands, by the grey sea
Eternal lies the city;
Upon the roof tops the fog
Weighs heavily,
And through the stillness of the city
Onward drones the sea.

Vienna was so different! And yet, this is the place we had been led to and where we had to accustom ourselves to a new way of life and a new kind of work.

The city of Aberdeen lies between the estuaries of the rivers Dee and Don. Five kilometres separate these two waterways where they now flow into the sea. Thousands of years ago they must have been united in a single delta which has since been gradually eroded by the North Sea. The River Dee springs from the Cairngorms — a region in the Scottish Highlands — and flows from west to east through the county of Aberdeenshire. The River Don, running north of the Dee, also has its source in the Cairngorms. To this day these two rivers still have a relationship to one another and they complement each other. The Dee is faster, friendlier and livelier. If the sun shines on its waters, the river smiles back and the salmon leap through its waves. The Don, however, is serious, slow and masculine in character, and flows through fields and meadows where there are fewer gardens and flowers along its banks; it has a more practical and pragmatic nature. According to legend, the great Columba wandered through the Dee Valley, preaching and evangelizing, and only from that time onwards did the land become fertile and abundant with flora. It is not known if this Irish monk's missionary extended to the banks of the River Don. Nevertheless, the remains of ancient stones circles and dolmens are embedded in the hills and knolls all around the Dee and Don. Everywhere one goes there is evidence of a prehistoric past. An ancient people was once settled there, most likely from the early and later Stone Age. Remains of their settlements have only recently been excavated on the Hebrides and Orkney Islands. Prehistoric dolmen, 'standing stones' and stone circles are still preserved at many sites.

The character of this landscape is infused with memory of an epoch in the earth's history when the Atlantis was destroyed and disappeared. It often rains for days on end here, and sometimes the sun is unable to break through the clouds and mist for weeks. As if in reminiscence, the days of flooding and progressive disintegration of the Atlantean continent are being repeated. Could the north of Scotland still be a last remaining limb of that ancient part of the earth that once sank into the flooding waters of the Atlantic Ocean?

The Ice Age and the early Stone Age with their megalithic monuments can still be experienced throughout this area. Even the local people — taciturn, ponderous and phlegmatic in their way — are still cave dwellers, that is, subconsciously and hidden behind the façade of modern daily life. They need a long time to accustom themselves to anything new. While visitors are warmly received, those who decide to settle there will rarely become one of them. It often takes generations for an outsider to be accepted into their social circles. It was much like that for us: They welcomed us warmly and were greatly accommodating, but the moment we made it known that we intended to settle there, nothing more than friendly politeness was forthcoming. Rejection and defensiveness grew behind the façade. Only a few people gave us a helping hand to further our activities — and there is still more to tell about them.

Since time immemorial there have been two cities in Aberdeen: Old Aberdeen is situated on the River Don and the Royal Borough of Aberdeen is to be found along the Dee. The name of the city was originally Aber-Don. I mention this because the two names Don and Donau (Danube), the main river flowing through Vienna, our former home city, resonate faintly with each other — and also with memories and homesickness. For centuries Old Aberdeen was the more exclusive and refined of the two cities. The atmosphere was reserved and conservative; a university was built there in 1495. Many eminent theologians and philosophers taught at this academy, amongst them Thomas Reid (1710–96), the founder of the Scottish School of Philosophy and renowned opponent of David Hume. The city of Aberdeen proper — the Borough of Aberdeen — is situated along the River Dee. It was the harbour city from the very beginning and this is where the different branches of trade and industry first developed. Although the Borough was also grey and misty, it was much more lively and relaxed than austere Old Aberdeen. Today the two cities merge into one and new buildings are scattered amongst the old. Almost all signs of individual character have disappeared into the bland modern architecture. The substance one could still sense and experience some twenty-five years ago now belongs to a lost and forgotten past.

Aberdeen is Protestant to the core, as is the case in many

The dee valley

northern countries. The Kirk — the Church — still has a certain influence on city life. The Church of Scotland is steeped in a kind of Puritanism which clearly bears traits of the dark times of Calvin and John Knox. Hardly a hymn is sung; not a decoration is to be seen — the church services consist only of preaching, prayer and Bible texts. Christianity has become a rigid belief system and the minister an 'employed' servant of the congregation.

The River Dee flows into the North Sea at the outskirts of the city. It is accompanied on its long journey by the Dee Valley, a narrow, fertile strip of land extending to the north and south. Small suburban settlements can be found along the banks of the river; further inland they are more village-like; there are also villas, country houses and farmhouses; here and there a street with shops and a few taverns. Camphill is situated on the north shore of the Dee, about 10 km upstream, in the hamlet of Milltimber.

Originally there were three houses — the large manor house, the so-called lodge (the porter's house where the gardener lived) and a small farmhouse with adjoining barns and stables. A horse and cart were kept for the ladies and gentlemen of the manor; there were also a few cows. Grass and oats were grown in the estate's fields and meadows, and the garden — enclosed within high walls — supplied vegetables for the small group of people who lived there. This was the situation when we took over the property around Whitsun 1940. At that time the large manor house had been occupied by a young, married couple without children. Camphill was for sale because they wanted to move to the city. The great park of the Camphill estate stretched as far as the banks of the River Dee — the melody of the river's murmuring flow always to be heard in the south-facing rooms. This song would only ever fall quiet in the winter when the Dee was slowed by ice floes.

The fields and meadows of a similar estate — called Maryculter — spread out on the opposite bank of the river in a slightly westerly direction. Both Camphill and Maryculter were once at the centre of a powerful estate encompassing many hundreds of hectares. On the perimeter of Maryculter, sheltered within the fences of an ancient cemetery, are the graves of the Templar Knights who once occupied this land. They had been the lords and gentlemen of that immense and powerful estate and they lived at Camphill and Maryculter. When we first arrived we were not aware that destiny had led us into this Templar past. It was only once we investigated the early history of Camphill that we discovered — with surprise and amazement — what a historical bastion had been handed on to us. Camphill had been one of the northernmost settlements of the Knights Templar Order. The last remaining ambassadors of the Order were also murdered here, as everywhere else in Europe.* Filled

* Recent research has shown that in contrast to France only three Templars in Scotland were tried, and none were executed. Many Scottish Knights Templar joined the Hospitallers and other the Order of Christ in Portugal.

with malicious intent and greed for gold treasure, Philippe the Fair, King of France, had vowed to destroy the Templars. When Jakob von Molay, the remaining Grand Master was burned at the stake on the Île de la Cité on the Seine in Paris, the great Order was finally wiped out. The last Camphill and Culter Templars would have been executed soon thereafter. The *auto-da-fé* was carried out on March 11, 1314. Hitler, as an imperator of horror, marched into Vienna and Austria on March 11, 1938. This was also when the history of the Camphill movement began.

I was born in Vienna at the beginning of this century [September 25, 1902]. My parents were Jewish; my father was of Burgenland descent and my mother came from Moravia. I was an only child and grew up in relative solitude. In some things I was rather headstrong and so my attendance of primary and secondary school was not without problems. Then the First World War arrived and brought along with it the fall of the Austro-Hungarian monarchy. I clearly remember the day when King Franz Joseph was entombed in the Capuchin crypt and then two years later — I was just sixteen years old — the collapse of the front and the November Revolution of 1918. At that time I became intensely occupied with philosophical, scientific and social questions: The loss of all previously existing values called for new norms and attitudes. In this striving, however, I had no support or guidance from my parents; moreover, as I was an only child, I had just a few friends. Therefore I was dependent upon books and without anyone to supervise me I studied the most colourful variety: Haeckel and Freud were read with the same devotion as George and Hofmannsthal, Buddha and Lao-tzu, Dumas and Balzac. Around this time I also discovered the New Testament and in this moment a whole new world opened up to the young boy. I felt I had met something that I had long been searching for and that my life would be deeply influenced by it from that point onwards. A second and significant source of education and guidance became available through my growing involvement with a group of young people who had formed a kind of Wandervogel association within the Austrian Socialist Youth movement. In this context I was directly confronted with social problems. I stepped into the realities of human society for the first time through my acquaintance with the young working class and our visits to the workers' colleges where I held talks and participated in discussions.

Some time later, the books and writings of Adolf Stöhr — who, at that time, was Professor of Philosophy and Psychology at the University of Vienna — introduced me to the questions of cognitive theory and the problems of sense-orientated perception. I was moved in the depths of my being by the riddle of the reality of the visible world, of the forming of ideas and imagination, and above all, by the process of thinking. For many days and nights I attempted to observe my thinking in order to find a clue to the process of acquiring knowledge. I was untiring in this quest; it preoccupied me constantly and incessantly during the last two years of my middle school years. Then came 1920, my final school year, and thereafter a preparatory year at the University of Vienna. As I had been in the *Realschule* [high school focused on science] I needed to catch up on Latin studies. Most important of all, however, I attended lectures on botany, zoology, experimental zoology and biology. The world of scientific research began to open itself to me forcefully. Once again I reached for all the books I could find, but as much as I was captivated by the wonders of the organic world, I was left dissatisfied with the attempts that had been made to explain them. Darwin, Haeckel, Driesch, Verworn, Von Uexküll, Hertwig and the many others that I studied showed possible paths of understanding, but I could not find either satisfactory or sufficiently extensive insights ... Until I found my way to Goethe's scientific writings.

His botanical and anthropological-morphological descriptions were like redemption for me. I felt directly addressed: these were the gateways that would lead to possible answers. In the Goethean conception of nature I met something that enlivened my thinking in the same way that the New Testament had awakened my senses for a new dimension of existence. Now, for the first time, the study of anatomy, embryology and histology could become a daily source of the most profound and heartfelt joy. Bones and muscles revealed new worlds to me. The idea of metamorphosis gripped my attention deeply, and through this I came to know the working of creative formative forces in nature. I also began to grasp the identity — the absolute 'oneness' — that exists between these creative forces and our thoughts. Outside in nature these formative forces work in such a way that they bring all organic forms into being, while inside, in the human soul, they are the creators of our thoughts and ideas. I began to write down an outline of these insights for my own reference. With regard to essential questions, however, I had the sense that I could hardly make myself understood to other people. In conversations and discussions with my few friends I continually encountered their complete incomprehension.

During this period — in about 1921 — I came across the name of Rudolf Steiner for the first time. While visiting an exhibition of modern paintings, I discovered a triptych by Richard Teschner, then a well-known Viennese painter and graphic artist. Confucius was depicted on the left hand side of the triptych; the meditating Buddha was on the right; and in the centre was the gaunt and ragged figure of a modern proletariat. A saying taken from the *Dhammapada* had been placed underneath the picture of the Buddha and a quotation from the *Lunyu* below the figure of Confucius. Beneath the central picture was a verse by Rudolf Steiner describing the dawning of a new age when souls would feel their bond with the spirit.

These words were spoken straight from the heart. But who indeed was this Rudolf Steiner who had been given a place beside the Buddha and Confucius? I obtained one of his books from the university library, *Goethe's World Conception.* Reading this book gave me a sense of deep fulfilment. But I was searching

Rudolf Steiner

for more: what was written there was already largely known to me ... Following a lecture at the university on the metamorphosis of bones given by Eugen Kolisko (who later became a friend), I came across a copy of Rudolf Steiner's book, *The Philosophy of Freedom.* That was it! Here I could read — often in the same words — what I myself had written about the creative forces in nature and human thinking! This was a deep and terrible shock for me. Had I somehow copied it all? Or was it a truth revealed to every searching thinker? The pathway to anthroposophy now opened up before me and I began to read Rudolf Steiner's seminal works. I never met him in person, however, and I missed the opportunity to hear him speak at the East-West Congress in Vienna in June 1922. My studies, a measure of youthful arrogance and also phlegma stood in my way. Later on I often and deeply regretted this, but perhaps it was also partly necessity that expressed itself in this turn of events.

Following the conclusion of the preliminary medical examinations, the clinical semesters commenced and at the same time I started work as an assistant at the university's Institute of Embryology in Vienna. Alfred Fischel was director of the Institute at the time and I considered him to be a good teacher, albeit somewhat pedantic. He and his colleagues held views on the mechanics of development similar to those established by Wilhelm Roux. Although we did not identify with one another, the three years spent at the Institute were of immense importance to me. I learned the methods of exact research and taught the art of using a microscope to hundreds of students. Most significant of all, however, I became thoroughly familiar with human embryo formation and development. Thus an abundant and unending source of new discoveries became available to me at the Institute and I was gradually able to develop new insights into the forces responsible for the formation of the human embryo. A major part of the literature on embryology at the Institute library was accessible and I particularly studied those works which presented the early stages of human embryo formation in a descriptive way. Then I made a significant discovery: The embryo's sheath organs form first of all; the embryo as such only begins to develop and build up itself later on. Of course, the developmental riddle that presented itself here provided the starting point for a spiritual scientific interpretation. I was able to show that the immense pictures presented in Genesis are mirrored and recapitulated in the phases of human embryonic sheath formation. The law of biogenetics — already no longer recognized at that time — could now be formulated in a new way. I was filled with a sense of deep satisfaction. For the first time the harmonious synthesis between science and anthroposophical spiritual science had revealed itself to me. This consideration of the 'whole' — the sum of the parts — became fundamental to my principles of work later on.

Around this time, on March 30, 1925, Rudolf Steiner passed away. The news shook me to the roots of my being: I felt numb in the face of this enormous loss. In summer that same year I travelled to Dornach for the first time and visited the centre of his work; it left a profound and lasting impression on me.

In clinical lectures [at the university] I learned about the diseased and ill human being; at the same time the perspectives and methods underlying the teaching repelled me. Also here the attempt was made to conceive of the human being in a purely material sense and any conclusions reached were consistent with this viewpoint. While patients were seldom truly healed, the prestigious reputation of the medical profession was nevertheless upheld. Some professors were good diagnosticians, illustrious surgeons and even witty conversationalists. But what remained of the 'true will to heal'? This had become an empty phrase that was convincingly paraded on memorial days and at graduation ceremonies. In fact, the sacred Hippocratic Oath had become a mere phantom of its original intention. Thus it also became necessary to search for new pathways in this sphere. Around that time I became associated with a small group of doctors and medical students motivated by anthroposophy and we took our first steps along this difficult road together. A large number of lectures given by Rudolf Steiner to interested doctors were already available. Although we devoted ourselves to their study, it took a long time for us to gain an understanding of Steiner's indications. I think about that group with much gratitude. The first foundations of my future medical work were laid in the process of our work together.

As the clinical semesters came to a conclusion, I had gained a preliminary overview of the medical field. I continued my work at the Institute of Embryology and published a small number of minor research studies. One study, however, was devoted to an experiment which aimed to prove the efficacy of homeopathically diluted substances. I was able to show that frog larvae went through quite differing processes of development and metamorphosis when subjected to homeopathic dilutions of silver and lead administered in increasing potency (D1 to D30). My lecture about this experiment at the Vienna Biology Society led to much lively debate. The following day I had to take my pharmacology examination, but the examiner, who had heard my lecture the previous evening, decided not to pass this rather poorly-prepared candidate. Nevertheless my research was published in the *Archiv für experimentelle Medizin* (Archive for Experimental Medicine), consequently supporting the cause for homeopathy. Also around that time the Bier Privy Council in Berlin stepped in to validate the efficacy of homeopathic medicines and the great conflict between conventional medicine and the Hahnemann students flared up once again.

I was awarded my medical doctorate in Vienna during spring 1927. Soon afterwards I went to work as an intern at a small hospital in Lower Austria where I was introduced to daily medical practice under the guidance of a kind and experienced senior consultant. The hospital was situated right next to the famous Klosterneuburg seminary — within the shadow of its buildings — and something of the peace and immanence of the Cistercian Order once at home there shone over us. I would sometimes sit in the seminary's large library and more often in the gardens where huge chestnut trees formed a canopy over the garden terrace. One could see as far as the Danube and across to the Marchfeld plain. At that time I became clearly conscious — as never before — of my Central European, Austrian identity.

ÜBER SYMMETRIE- UND LÄNGENVERHÄLTNISSE DER VERKNÖCHERTEN SKELETTEILE MENSCHLICHER EMBRYONEN

VON

K. KÖNIG UND W. KORNFELD

MIT 4 TEXTABBILDUNGEN UND 1 TAFEL

SONDERDRUCK
AUS DER
ZEITSCHRIFT
FÜR ANATOMIE UND ENTWICKLUNGSGESCHICHTE
(I. ABTEILUNG DER ZEITSCHRIFT FÜR DIE GESAMTE ANATOMIE)
HERAUSGEGEBEN VON
E. KALLIUS
82. BAND, HEFT 6

J. F. BERGMANN UND JULIUS SPRINGER
MÜNCHEN BERLIN
1927

König's research paper on the symmetry and proportions of the skeleton of human embryos

In autumn the same year a crucial change came about in my life which resulted in my absence from my home country for many years. Soon after receiving my doctorate I was asked to deliver a science lecture as part of a public anthroposophical congress (I had become a member of the General Anthroposophical Society in 1925). So I chose the subject of Haeckel and the evolution of organisms and the biogenetic law (the exact formulation of the title, however, escapes my memory now). The lecture, held in a great hall, earned me considerable recognition and members of the Anthroposophical Society began to be aware of me. At the same time, Professor Fischel, then Dean of the Medical Faculty offered me a post-doctoral position at the Institute of Embryology and promised me his full support. I drew his attention to my anthroposopical views, but he was of the opinion that as long I did not present these in my lectures at the university, nothing would stand in the way of my 'private' affinities. I could not agree to this and consequently took leave of my association with the Institute. Shortly afterwards I concluded my work at Klosterneuburg, and took up a position as a senior houseman at one of the large children's hospitals in the suburbs of Vienna in order to further my medical studies in paediatrics.

Ita Wegman visited Vienna in October 1927. This great personality had been Rudolf Steiner's closest collaborator during the last years of his life. At the time of her visit she was director of the Clinical Therapeutic Institute in Arlesheim near Basle, a nursing home affiliated to the Goetheanum and the School for Spiritual Science, and also leader of the School's Medical Section. I was introduced to her at a social event and in the conversation that followed she invited me to work as an assistant doctor at her clinic. After some initial hesitation, I willingly accepted her offer. I had already sensed that my time in Vienna had come to an end: The public lecture had concluded this period in my life and my departure from the Institute of Embryology further confirmed this turn of events. I spoke to my parents, informed my friends and then travelled to Basle —

without a contract of employment or even a work permit, but with a sense of trust that good fortune was on my side. I arrived at Arlesheim on the evening of November 6 and on November 7 I celebrated the start of my new job at the Clinical Therapeutic Institute. A new phase of my life began.

Rudolf Steiner gave a series of twelve lectures on curative education only months before his death, between June 24 and July 7, 1924, in response to the request of a few of young people who, having chosen the field of curative education and care of children with special needs as their life's work, were dissatisfied with prevailing methodology and practice. By this time a branch of the Clinical Therapeutic Institute in Arlesheim already cared for a small number of children with special needs. Moreover, only a few weeks before the beginning of this course, the first 'Curative and Educational Institute for Children with Special Needs' had been established in Jena. It was called Lauenstein. During a visit to Lauenstein on June 18, Rudolf Steiner expressed his satisfaction with the way in which the institute had been established and consequently promised to give a series of lectures on curative education. This, in fact, is how the course came about. It became the seed — a source of life — for a curative education movement that would be carried by Ita Wegman's worldwide initiative for nearly two decades.

Initially, a number of smaller and larger institutions sprang up in Germany, England and Switzerland where children with all kinds of special needs received medical treatment, guidance and education according to Rudolf Steiner's indications. Thus a completely new way of caring for children with special needs became active in the world. These human beings were no longer seen as inferior, and they now received their full share of all the love and devotion that they needed. The original curative education impulses of Itard, Séguin, Pestalozzi and Guggenbühl at the beginning of the nineteenth century were taken up once again — now illuminated and elucidated by the potent insights of spiritual science.

As soon as I had somewhat settled in at Arlesheim, Dr Wegman invited me to the Sonnenhof. Situated at the rear of Arlesheim Cathedral she had acquired and developed for the purpose of curative educational work. She acquainted me with her special charges and problem children and asked me if I would be interested in this kind of work. I was certainly taken by surprise by this question. Dr Wegman was an impulsive personality, and often acted out of immediate inspirations and ideas. I was faced with a completely new world here. I had encountered the problems of these children only twice before and both times they had made an impression on me — although not to the extent that a destiny-determining impulse had grown in me. When I was a child, a family relative (on my father's side), who was both deaf and mute sometimes visited us. I watched her gesticulations and her sad inability to speak with a child's pain. Later on, as a secondary school student, there was an occasion when I was obliged to go for a walk with a mentally impaired boy, the son of my parents' friends. He was about my age. Our conversation unfolded falteringly: He was searching to make a connection, but my heart was closed to his wishes. But here at the Sonnenhof, there were about thirty smaller and bigger children with enormous or tiny heads, with paralysed limbs; some with an empty gaze; others traumatized by fits. But all of them were children! They laughed and cried; they were joyful and suffered pain like all other children. I was struck deeply and immediately by two things: The 'humanity' in each single one of these odd souls and the host of morphological deformations and flaws of nature that confronted me. 'Through these imperfections,' I said to myself, 'you will be able to research the hidden mysteries of development in the human form.'

Consequently, when Dr Wegman asked me if I would be prepared to spend a part of my day working at the Sonnenhof as a doctor, I willingly agreed. I was instantly drawn to these children and they quickly became very dear to me. And so I spent many hours with them, learning to dress and undress them, to clean them, to play with them, to calm or encourage them, and to be their friend. I spent another part of my day in the Clinic's laboratory working on experiments that were not of much use at the time. I also participated in artistic and curative eurythmy courses and treated individual patients.

The first Advent Sunday soon arrived, a festival that had been completely unknown to me in Catholic Vienna, and one I had never before celebrated. In the afternoon I went to the Sonnenhof to be with the children and there I found a group of co-workers and children gathered together. They sat along the walls in the biggest room in the house. In the middle of the space there was a small mound made out of green moss and earth and a candle was burning on top of it. A spiral marked out with moss lead to the small mound. Every child was given an apple upon which a small candle was fixed. Advent and Christmas songs were sung and one child after another attempted — alone or with help — to walk through the moss spiral to reach the central mound so that they could light their own candle from the main candle. I was profoundly surprised to behold the earnestness and joy with which each child approached the task. There was the great candle! Each small candle attached to an 'apple of sin' had to be lit from this 'proclaiming' Christmas light! And suddenly I knew: Yes, this is my future task! To awaken in each one of these children their own spirit light which would lead them to their humanity: yes, that is what I want to do! I am no longer able to say whether my decision was particularly conscious that Advent Sunday but my heart felt so fulfilled that tears just poured from my eyes and I had to leave the hall. Since then these people have been my *raison d'être.*

During the course of these days Dr Wegman quite suddenly asked me if I would be prepared to give a lecture at the coming Christmas Conference at the Goetheanum. I readily agreed — although today I cannot say where I found the courage to do so. I walked around 'pregnant' with the lecture content during all of Advent. I intended to speak about human embryo sheaths and to

Ita Wegman at the Sonnenhof

describe how their process of development paralleled the six days of creation in Genesis. My preparation was accompanied by the image of Raphael's Sistine Madonna — in her I saw an artistic enhancement of the human embryo sheaths. The Jesus child in her arms carried the imprint of the incarnating soul that is striving towards the earth. This lecture was a great success. I spoke to about one thousand people in the Schreinerei (the carpentry workshop) which was still being used as an improvised lecture hall following the burning of the first Goetheanum during New Year's Night, 1922/23. As a result of this lecture, numerous invitations came my way to hold lectures at different cities in Switzerland and Germany. I remember the overcrowded hall at the Bernoullianum in Basle; the Stuttgart branch auditorium filled to capacity; and the lecture halls in Jena, Leipzig and Berlin. I had become a speaker overnight, yet I did not understand how this had happened.

My memories about the Jena lectures are still quite clear. Fired with great purpose and determination, I delivered my address about Haeckel and biogenetic law to a public audience. Most important of all, however, I visited the Lauenstein Institute which, by then, had given birth to another curative education institute called Zwätzen. There I developed beautiful friendships with Franz Löffler who had been part of the group instrumental in bringing about the Curative Education Course and also with the resident doctor, Dr Heinrich Hardt. As a result of Franz Löffler's shared devotion to the great individuality of Ernst Haeckel, I began to gain some understanding of the background to Rudolf Steiner's comments regarding this personality and his link to Jena and the curative work developing there.

Before Whitsun 1928 came around, I once again set off on a lecture tour, this time to Breslau and Vienna. But first, the story of events leading up to this journey must be told. On November 7, 1927 — the day of my arrival in Arlesheim — I met the person who was living in an attic room of the same house I had just moved into. This was Miss Tilla Maasberg, who, together with her sister, Maria, had recently established a small curative education institute in the Silesian Eulengebirge. They had been joined by Albrecht Strohschein, another member of the group responsible for initiating the Curative Education Course. Seeds of the original Lauenstein impulse had begun to drift on the wind in every direction and to take root in new and different places. Tilla Maasberg had come to the Arlesheim clinic with the intention of taking training courses in painting, lyre playing, curative eurythmy and so on, and thus preparing herself for future curative work. As she was a graduated paediatric nurse she had already acquired comprehensive background training. We understood each other. We were also the same age and through her I came to know an aspect of German culture, which, as an Austrian, had so far eluded me. Through many conversations a beautiful friendship grew between us. Unfortunately she had to break off her training prematurely and return to Silesia soon

Albrecht Strohschein, Maria Maasberg, Hermann Kirchner, Sister Annegret, H. Weiss, Mrs Strohschein, Tilla Maasberg

after Christmas. Her help was needed at the curative home and her sister, Lena, was seriously ill. She hoped very much that I would help her sister medically and at the same time I would see her home and acquaint myself with the curative work being established there. Of course, it was the invitation to lecture at Breslau that enabled me to realize this visit.

A few months later I travelled to Silesia, gave the promised lectures at Breslau and then went on to Gnadenfrei to visit Miss Maasberg and her ill sister. The new children's home, Waldhaus, was close by. An extraordinary event awaited me at Gnadenfrei

— an experience that rooted itself in the depths of my soul and became a formative influence on my further destiny. What I encountered there was not yet known to me, but even so, strings began to vibrate within me, drawing out melodies which had never before resounded in my inner world. At that time Gnadenfrei was still a small village; a self-contained island adjacent to the market towns of Ober- and Niederpeilan at Reichenbach. It still had much of its original character, probably still from the time when it was first established in the mid-eighteenth century. Gnadenfrei was typical of the settlements built by the Herrnhuter, a brotherhood originally founded by Count Zinzendorf. At the large square there were two mighty residential buildings; one for the brothers and another for the sisters. There was also a church — its interior still bright, refined and quiet. I was deeply moved by the simple, solemn atmosphere that filled this space. The Table of the Lord was positioned higher than the rows of congregation benches. It was surrounded by a gallery and the high windows brought bright light flooding into this true House of God. 'How beautiful,' I thought to myself, and I was filled with a great joy. God's acre — the cemetery — lay behind the village and was surrounded by tall trees. Broad pathways led to the graves: Each had a headstone; none was any larger than the other. Everyone is equal in death! Here too an earnest and dignified mood reigned; there was no evidence of pomp and pageantry. 'Yes,' I thought, 'this is the way that life and death should be carried in a community of human beings.' The encounter was graced and I was filled with joyful amazement when I realized the significance of this event. Rarely had a place and its atmosphere affected me so directly.

Tilla Maasberg's family received me warmly. I visited her sister, Lena, spoke to her parents and then we travelled up to the Waldhaus where Mr Strohschein and Maria Maasberg welcomed me. I also met the children and felt immediately at home with them. The next day was Ascension. Following a morning celebration together with the children, we went on a tour

Eine Heilpädagogische Provinz.
Die pädagogische Provinz.
~~Die pädagogische~~ Provinz .
(Erster Entwurf.)

Dr.K.König u. Albrecht Strohschein

Als vor mehr als hundert Jahren Johann Gottlieb Fichte seine Reden an die deutsche Nation hielt,schloss er die letzte dieser Reden mit einer gewaltigen Mahnung. Er sprach:" Die alte Welt mit ihrer Herrlichkeit und Grösse,sowie mit ihren Mängeln ist versunken durch die eigne Unwürde und durch die Gewalt eurer Väter. Jst in dem,was in diesen Reden dargelegt worden,Wahrheit,so seid unter allen neueren Völkern ihr es,in dem der Keim der menschlichen Vervollkommnung am Entschiedensten liegt und denen Vorschritt in der Entwickelung derselben aufgetragen ist. Gehet ihr in dieser eurer Wesenheit zugrunde,so geht mit Euch zugleich alle Hoffnung des gesamten Menschengeschlechtes auf Rettung aus der Tiefe seiner Uebel zugrunde."

Mit diesen Worten schloss Fichte seinen gewaltigen Aufruf an die Deutschen. Er wollte damit erreichen,dass das deutsche Volk seine Aufgabe,die es als geistige Nation in dem darauf folgenden Jahrhundert hätte erfüllen müssen,klar erkenne. Er wollte,dass das deutsche Volk eine geistige Nation werde,nicht eine physische Nationalität, eine geistige Nation,aus welcher die Kraft erwachsen sollte,den Völkern der Erde in den kommenden Jahren der Versuchungen,Verführungen und Enttäuschungen, den richtigen Weg zu wahren. Heute wissen wir alle,dass der Mahnruf umsonst war.

Auch als Goethe, etwa um die gleiche Zeit versuchte,das Willensfeuer Fichtes,das die Herzen der deutschen Nation hätte entzünden sollen,in klare Jdeen einzuspannen und als die Jdee des kommenden Deutschlands die pädagogische Provinz darstellte,wurde er nicht verstanden; über Goethe und Fichte schwang die Historie die Fahne. Beide Männer wurden zerpflückt und zerschlagen durch die intellektuellen Aus-

König and Strohschein's manuscript on curative education

through the children's home and the beautiful park. We spoke a great deal about curative educational work and I was asked if I would be prepared to work there as a doctor. I expressed my willingness, but said that a larger house would have to found in order to generate enough work. And then just on that day, after lunch the visitors arrived, Mr and Mrs von Jeetze. They owned a huge estate close to a small town called Striegau. They could no longer afford to maintain the estate and had come to ask Mr Strohschein if he would take on the Pilgramshain Castle and its estate. They were willing to make these buildings and grounds available for curative educational work. This was an immediate and direct response to the condition I had only just set! Destiny had spoken swiftly and decisively. The experience of the brotherhood, carried in my innermost heart, had prepared the way for me to recognize this clear sign of human destiny. I said 'Yes,' and the co-workers decided to take on Pilgramshain Castle in summer of the same year. I promised to return in September and to start work together with my colleagues.

I stopped in Prague and Vienna on my return journey to Arlesheim. On Whitmonday I was asked to give another lecture at the Schreinerei in Dornach. The young 'upstart,' however, met the strong opposition of a group of people who wanted to make his life difficult within the Anthroposophical Society. This is another long chapter that affected the founding of Camphill indirectly and for that reason is only mentioned briefly here.

In the summer [of 1928], I travelled to Holland and England together with Dr Wegman and a great number of friends. The first larger anthroposophical medical clinic in Holland, founded by Dr Zeylmans van Emmichoven, was to be opened in the Hague. Along with other doctors, I was also invited to give an address at this event. In London we attended the World Conference for Anthroposophy which had been called by Dr Wegman. A whole host of leading anthroposophists gathered for the event at the Friends House, a large Quaker Centre. Consequently I was able to meet many significant individuals.

Amongst them was the founder of the Christian Community, Friedrich Rittelmeyer; the poet Fritz Lemmermeyer, a friend of Rudolf Steiner in his youth; Daniel N. Dunlop, the Chairman of the Anthroposophical Society in Great Britain and of the important World Conference; Dr Walter Johannes Stein, Dr Eugen Kolisko, Dr Karl Schubert and Caroline von Heydenbrandt, who were Waldorf teachers; Dr Eberhard Schickler, the Stuttgart doctor, and many others. I developed profound, life-long friendships with some of these individuals later on. These days in London became a great celebration of spiritual life in Central Europe. Out of their striving to work with the 'spirit' of the century, a group of people declared to the British public — in the centre of London — their faith and hope in the 'seed of spirituality' that Rudolf Steiner had sown. This was one of the last great events before the barbarism of 1933 took hold and a 'dark night of the spirit' fell upon Central Europe. This was my first glimpse of life in the British Empire. At that time I did not know that it would become my new home within a few years. In looking back, however, it seems that this World Conference was like a motif which first sounded softly and then was the very substance I worked with to bring the Camphill movement into being ten years later.

From London I made my return journey to Arlesheim where I look my leave of Dr Wegman and the clinic. Then I travelled on to Vienna to see my parents and arrived at Pilgramshain at the beginning of September. Tilla Maasberg was waiting for me at the railway station at Striegau. A period of intensive work and organizational development now began. Pilgramshain rapidly expanded into a large curative education institute: Within less than two years we were already caring for more than a hundred children and teenagers. At first the Welfare Department for Youth in Berlin, sent maladjusted children and teenagers to us, and also those with behavioural problems. Furthermore, we had taken into our care a substantial group of children with more specific and severe special needs. Hence a multifaceted task confronted us. We attempted to modify the old house — originally built for quite other purposes — so that it would gradually meet the new requirements. Despite our best intentions, however, we were still beginners in this work and so we were only partially successful in what we had set out and undertaken to accomplish.

Many other tasks and responsibilities soon came to the fore, however, and before long I had to withdraw from the actual curative work. A substantial part of my time was occupied with intensive lecturing in Lower Silesia, Bohemia and Berlin. Above all, though, an ever increasing number of patients came to me wanting advice and help. People travelled from all over; arriving by train and car, by bus and van. Aristocracy and workers, farmers and town-dwellers all sat peaceably together in the waiting rooms. When I had to leave Pilgramshain in 1936 because of political pressures, I reviewed my patient records and realized that during these seven years I had treated some 40,000 patients. In the beginning, the curative educational work had, in fact, been the framework for this diversity of professional activities. Certainly, I learned about many different irregularities and deformations of human development but I did not have enough time, peace and quiet or the possibility for the intensity of effort which would be necessary to deepen and thoroughly work through the images that had come to me regarding the different human conditions. The number of patients increased to such a degree and the onrush of work so pressurized me that I had to consider changing my working circumstances. At the same time, living conditions steadily worsened for the Jews in Germany. By then I had three children — Tilla Maasberg had become my wife on May 5, 1929 — and I had to think about their future. Consequently, I returned to Vienna at the end of 1935. At the beginning of March 1936 I went with my family to visit friends in Prague and Bohemia, and on May 1 we moved into a rented house in a suburb of Vienna. I returned to Vienna at the end of 1935, leaving my family behind. Then at the beginning of March

1936 I went back for my family, and on May 1 we moved into a rented house in a suburb of Vienna.

In retrospect, I consider the work I accomplished in Silesia to be an outcome of my earliest beginnings in curative education. I did not engage with this task to the fullest possible extent at the time. Instead, I had become a doctor who had developed a particular capacity to recognize unique qualities in the individual patient. My will to heal strengthened and my enthusiasm achieved a great deal (albeit that I did not yet have sufficient knowledge or skills). I became aware that this attitude was of fundamental importance for the interaction between doctor and patient. Guided by Rudolf Steiner's indications and brilliant conceptions, my insights into the nature of illness grew. As a doctor, I also succeeded to some extent in 'passing nature's examinations': herb and stone, metal and animal substances became known to me as medicines; I learned how to administer them according to the individual illness. However, a full and proper commitment to curative education had not been fulfilled and the strong social impulse that I had carried since my youth had also not come to expression. Moreover, the experience of brotherhood founded on the basis of faith — which I had for the first time at Gnadenfrei and then ever more frequently — had also not come to any practical fruition or transformation. Not that I had this insight at the time; this only became clear to me when I looked back on my life. I returned to Vienna to escape the political crisis that had begun Germany. At first, this seemed to be the simplest and most feasible way forward open to me and my family. Once in Vienna, I attempted nothing more than to build up a medical practice. I could envision nothing further in that moment. But the old and new ideals lived on in my soul and I seldom gave up the hope that a curative education working community could be established in the future. Destiny ordained that the short period of time given to me in Vienna would be a preparation phase. In somewhat less than 28 months the essential work had to be accomplished, for already in August 1938 I

KARL KÖNIG
(in Österreich approbierter Arzt)
SCHLOSS PILGRAMSHAIN

STRIEGAU-LAND, am
Fernruf 384

26. Februar 1936

Liebe Freunde!

Heute, am Vorabend von Dr Steiners 75. Geburtstag, möchte ich den Abschied aus der Reihe der in der Heilpädagogik tätigen Menschen nehmen. Vor 8 Jahren trat ich in diesen Kreis. Heute scheide ich daraus, durch mancherlei innere u äußere Ereignisse, dazu gezwungen. Die Arbeit am Aufbau des Pilgramshainer Institutes war ein Teil meiner Lebensarbeit. Überschaue ich es jetzt, so waren es meine Lehrjahre u ich hoffe, dass nun die Wanderjahre beginnen können. Diese Lehrjahre sind voll der glücklichsten u schmerzlichsten Erlebnisse. Der Aufschwung der heilpädagogischen Arbeit, die grossen Tagungen in Hamburg u Berlin, in London sind unvergesslich. Die vielerlei Arbeiten mit hunderten Menschen, die innerstes Interesse an unserem Werk hatten, gehören zu dem Schönen. Die Stunden der Andacht in der ärztlichen Sorge um die Kinder zu dem Innigsten in der Erinnerung. Schmerzlich sind die mehr „internen" Erlebnisse. Das immer wiederkehrende Versagen der menschlichen Gemeinschaft innerhalb des Institutes u zwischen den Instituten. Die eigene Selbstgefälligkeit u die der Freunde. Die vielen Scheuklappen vor der Welt in unseren Reihen u jetzt das Verlassen-Sein von allem, was noch vor Monaten das innerste Leben bedeutet hat.

Ich möchte Ihnen mitteilen, dass ich zunächst für einige Monate in die Tschecho-Slowakei gehe u dort mit einigen Ärzten (etwa 25) intensiv anthroposophisch zu arbeiten.

Anschließend daran (am 1. August 1936) werde ich mich in Wien als Arzt niederlassen, um zunächst in aller Stille u. Bescheidenheit verschiedene Dinge zu verfolgen, die mir wichtig erscheinen.

Ich werde sehr froh sein, ~~von~~ wenn einmal der eine oder andere von Ihnen sich so an mich erinnert, daß er mich etwas vom Leben in den Instituten wissen läßt.

Ich wünsche allen eine gedeihliche Arbeit u. den Segen der göttliche Mächte.

Dr König

König's valedictory review of his time in Pilgrimshain (translation, see pages 82f).

was forced to flee from my home country. From there the road led directly to Scotland.

I was 34 years old when I moved into the house in Vienna together with my family. Thus it happened that I spent the mid-point of my life — the thirty-fifth year — in the city of my birth. This became the most intense period of work I had ever experienced. My actual existence, however, in spite of the presence of my wife and children, was reduced virtually to zero. Everything in my life seemed to have contracted into a tight knot. What had already been achieved was no longer visible or active in the world: Pilgramshain, the large and faithful circle of patients, the lecturing activities — all had come to an end. I was alone and reliant only upon myself. Forced to start over, I now had to carve out a completely new basis for my existence. This was a good training in the practicalities of life and in learning to trust in the spirit. But it was difficult in the beginning. Quite some time passed before the first patients arrived and sometimes I did not know where the money would come from for our daily needs; yet we seldom went hungry. For many months, however, only the essentials of daily life were available to us. Then, in autumn 1936, a larger number of patients began to visit the practice and already by Christmas that year I needed the help of a second doctor.

Knowing that medicines alone would not be sufficient, I also began to hold lectures for the patient circle. Ever-increasing numbers came to these evenings, including some younger people who attended regularly. During my previous visits to Vienna, I had also become acquainted with another small but special group of young people — students and others — who wanted to undertake an in-depth study of spiritual science. This group was imbued with an odd mix of melancholy and true spiritual striving which was deeply embedded in their young souls. In order to meet their needs I certainly had to practice a great deal of reserve and learn how to be tactful in human relationships. The lecture evenings soon generated a second group asking for more than a general introduction to anthroposophy. These were well-educated, affluent young people who had discovered something deeply interesting and appealing to them through my presentation of spiritual science. I attempted to bring these two destiny groups together: the bourgeois, melancholic group who seemed much older in demeanour; and the new arrivals with their *savoir vivre* and zest for life. It was not easy to find a common basis. During Advent, however, when we studied the Oberufer Nativity play together, the simple piety and devotional quality of the images and words forged a mutual soul connection between them. From this moment on a certain degree of social unity was established. Now the common work could begin. Of course, at that time I did not know that the core of Camphill would form itself out of this group. So this is how the future prepared itself in 'seed' form — within only a few short months of my return to Vienna.

We chose as our first theme of study the work and biographies of individuals who had died early on in the World War: Bernhard von der Marwitz, Otto Braun, Franz Marc, August Macke and others. We sensed that these young people had attempted to prepare the ground for something we should continue. Thus we found our way into the stream of historical evolution. We did not want to remain on the fringes of this endeavour, but wished, on the contrary, to be part of making one of Central Europe's tasks become reality. These conversations and studies also gave us the opportunity to explore different aspects of spiritual science. Questions about reincarnation and karma and the existence of a life between death and a new birth could also be addressed. The individual human biographical phenomena provided us with a means to work through the general, fundamental principles of anthroposophy. It was deeply satisfying for me to witness how active their spiritual striving became. Every now and again their understanding of the existence of a spiritual world and the effects of spiritual beings would deepen and intensify. This process prepared the way for the study of a series of lectures given by Rudolf Steiner to a group of young people in 1922, some fifteen years earlier. The Pedagogical Youth Course contained many suggestions relevant to our intentions. As a consequence of our study, we awoke to a realization amongst ourselves: we not only wanted to acquire knowledge of anthroposophy, but most important of all, our striving was about actively taking on the task of planting seeds of renewal into Central Europe's declining civilization. This could not happen through knowledge alone. What was needed was active, spiritually-sustained work — deeds which would flow from the whole of the human being and not only as part of a 'career.' We also felt this should not be accomplished by someone alone but rather communally, by a group of people. At first these impressions could not be precisely formulated. We expressed it amongst ourselves by saying, more or less: We do not only want to study anthroposophy; we want it to be part of our lives and work. Some of Rudolf Steiner's words were a great help to us because, again and again, he pointed to this 'active work arising from anthroposophy.'

And so, the first months of 1937 went by. The patient community grew rapidly and before long the waiting room would fill up to such an extent that I was often unable to see all the ill people. The practice also became a so-called *Praxis aurea* amongst circles of nobility and prominent people in industry and politics whose closest representatives often consulted me. Actors, authors and artists also sought my medical advice. This work became so demanding that there was little time left for private study. Nevertheless, I met a great number and variety of people, and I was forced to realize — with confusion and amazement — that even the best-informed were blind to what was actually happening in Central Europe. They all hoped that it 'would not be too bad.' And every day I had to think of the Greek truism, 'the gods make blind those whom they wish to destroy.'

Most of us went on holiday during the summer. I spent ten

days in southern Bohemia at the Hohenfurth Monastery in Krumau [now Moravsky Krumlov in the Czech Republic] as a guest of the abbot who was a patient of mine. I mention this visit because it enabled me to deeply absorb an experience of Adalbert Stifter's home country for one last time. I visited Oberplan and Rosenberg, and devoutly re-read some of his studies and the novel, *Nachsommer* [Indian Summer]. Thus an impulse strengthened within me that was to contribute substantially to the founding and establishment of Camphill. The profound respect for the human being; for the active laws of nature; and the attention to detail — these were the fundamental principles of our way of life later on.

We all came together again in the early autumn, now venturing into new and varied activities. The young friends had travelled far and wide; some had been at the World Exhibition in Paris; others in Italy. As the youth group grew in numbers yet again, we had to move the weekly lecture venue to a large hall in the city centre. A doctors' group came into being and the already too-large patient community continued to increase daily. Thus I became surrounded by an abundance of life, destinies and varied work. The general mood, however, had changed completely. Now people were filled with deep-seated resignation. Doom and destruction threatened the one; the other hoped that salvation would come from northern countries. At that time I treated a large number of 'secret' (Nazi) party members in the police and high level office, and consequently became aware of much more than I actually wanted to know. I refrained from taking up any opportunities that this situation presented because I did not want to withdraw from the fate that was now inevitably approaching the group of young friends.

At Christmas time we performed the Oberufer Nativity play and also a dramatic piece on the creation of Adam and his expulsion from Paradise. Many hundreds of people took part in the event. The following Holy Nights were quiet and graced. Then destiny struck, sudden and uncompromising. For some hours on January 25, 1938 the mighty aurora borealis transformed the entire night sky across Europe into flaming red. This seemed to be a portent pleading with humankind to be conscious and to reflect. But only a few heard the voice calling as the Baptist did: 'Change your ways!' Some days later Hitler demanded the presence of the Austrian Chancellor at Berchtesgaden where he humiliated and insulted him most grievously. At that point we all sensed that the end was near. With the prey already between its jaws, the beast now just played with its life before devouring it completely. Nevertheless I continued to hold lectures and the youth group went on meeting with undiminished strength. We waited to see what would happen. As war could have broken out any day then, our feelings continually wavered between hope and resignation. Yet the heart beat steadily on, giving us courage and trust. What could possibly happen to us? We were together!

Austria fell on March 11, 1938 under the pressure of propaganda attacks from outside and betrayal from within by our so-called 'fellow countrymen.' The German troops crossed the borders and the government was forced to relinquish power. It was a pitiful and disreputable end. Thoroughly corrupt through slander and lies, Austria could offer no resistance and was defeated. On the evening of that very day, our youth group came together. We read the last lecture of the Pedagogical Youth Course where Rudolf Steiner speaks about the working of the Archangel Michael in the twentieth century, calling on young people to make it possible for Michael to penetrate through the death and decay of contemporary civilization.

> The Age of Michael — he who conquers the dragon — must begin, for the power of the dragon has become great! This is what we have to achieve, however, if we want to provide the right kind of guidance for our young people. Michael needs, as it were, a vehicle to enter our civilization. And this vehicle can be uncovered by the

> true educator — if it emerges amongst the youth, the children — the 'becoming' human being. Strength from the pre-earthly life is still working in them. If we provide the right kind of education we prepare a vehicle for Michael to enter and penetrate our civilization.[1]

Yes, what was expressed here lived in our hearts as a longing. This was what really mattered to us and what we were striving to achieve. We were surrounded by chaos, madness and destruction and yet a light that we could follow with courage and good conscience had begun to shine in us. The closing words of the lecture gave us strength and guidance.

> The above observations were meant in the sense that, rather than carrying what I have said here in your heads and thinking about it, I wish you to have something in your hearts, and transform what is in your hearts into effective action. What we carry in our heads is lost along the way. What we take into our hearts, however, the heart will safeguard in whatever situations and spheres of action we are placed in.[2]

Those were the very words we needed that night. They gave us purpose, strength and direction for what our future should become. We — those present — promised ourselves that we would faithfully carry our resolution to build a vehicle for Michael — wherever that may be — which he could use to enter our civilization. With this promise we took our leave of one another. We did not know if we would remain free from harm or when we could meet again.

Outside the city was raging; Hitler youth in their white stockings, men in brown uniforms, and screeching women all danced around the dragon. Yet in the midst of this insane commotion a flame had been kindled; a flame that was to forge a sword of peace that could, perhaps, also shine as a small light for future deeds. For behind the veil, hidden in the background of this event, was the blazing fire of the funeral pyre upon which Jakob von Molay was burned to death some 624 years earlier.* These flames and those of the other fires that consumed the bodies of the Templars emblazoned the night sky on January 25 — because this Order had been in the service of Michael.

During the following days it seemed as if Vienna and her people were drunk. And just as it is with a state of intoxication, half the people laughed hysterically and the other half was overwhelmed with misery. There was something strange and cruel about having to continue to live daily life in such catastrophic conditions. I was often called out as a doctor during these days to attend to suicide cases amongst my patients. They opened gas taps, threw themselves onto the streets from the top floors of their houses, overdosed on morphine or even shot themselves and their families. One despairing act followed another, and the 'victors' did everything to intensify fear and confusion. They confiscated homes and publicly ridiculed and degraded people on the streets. The victims' fear was so great that they complied without a word. And it was through this utterly blatant display of brutality that another aspect of the Austrian nation started to become clearly visible. I too was seized by the epidemic of panic during these days. I saw how everything I had achieved — a growing seed — was collapsing into nothing around me. But my courageous and loyal wife stood by me and within a few hours I had surmounted this crisis.

My friends did not come to any harm and nor was their freedom compromised at any time. Moreover, my family and I were able to continue daily life without too much humiliation. The medical practice also remained unharmed. Nonetheless, each one of us knew that if we wanted to keep our promise we would have to emigrate as quickly as possible. But where were we to go? By that time German and Austrian refugees were no longer accepted by many European countries — they too were in

* Jakob von Molay, the last Grand Master of the Order of Templars, was burned in Paris in 1314.

imminent danger of becoming the raging dragon's next victims. As we did not want to be drawn into the approaching war, we searched for a place where, in spite of the pending catastrophe, we could begin to develop our work. At the same time we did not want to leave Europe because we were not yet prepared to flee. Consequently the Irish Republic was our first choice and we also considered Cyprus because refugees were still being received there. We believed that the governments concerned should be fully informed as to our intentions, and so, following many shared conversations and discussions with the friends of the youth group, I wrote 'a plan for the establishment of a curative education institute.' This document contained the basic principles for such an institute, which, in part at least, we were able to realize later on. Our plan had been written with the contemporary situation in mind and formulated in such a way as to meet the conditions required by Ireland. Those who try to recall the situation in Europe in spring 1938 would have to consider our project as pure illusion. For at that time every European country blocked all possible paths to emigration. And now an entire group of people, most of them young and without a real profession or practical training wanted to start anew somewhere — albeit with a very unusual project. 'This cannot possibly be realized now' was the daily assessment of the situation; 'it is an impossible undertaking!'

The Irish Government refused our application almost immediately; there was no reply from Cyprus. What was to be done now? Surprisingly, we never once became dejected. We had firm faith in our idea and most of us were absolutely determined to follow it through to its practical realization somewhere in Europe. And so the group devised the following plan: Each one of us would make an independent attempt to escape entrapment in Austria; we would do everything to keep strong and true bonds to each other; and the first of us to discover a situation where we could potentially realize our plans would inform the others. This is how we ensured a common path of action.

Anhang I.

Genauer Plan zur Errichtung eines heilpädagogischen Institutes in Südirland.

Seit in der menschlichen Kultur-Entwicklung, Siedlungs-Gemeinschaften zu entstehen begonnen haben, wurden in diesen Niederlassungen immer wieder Menschen geboren, die durch bestimmte Abnormitäten, (die nicht in das eigentliche Gebiet des Krankseins gehören, da die Krankheit ein vorübergehendes Ereignis darstellt) auffielen. Abnormitäten, die sich vor allem darin kundtun, dass diese Menschen nicht fähig waren, einer normalen Gemeinschaft eingegliedert zu werden. Und es war immer Brauch, dass die (betreffende) menschliche Siedlung für diese abnormen Menschen gemeinschaftlich sorgte.

So lange der Mensch ein Jäger war, solange also die Siedlungs-Gemeinschaften noch keinen festen Wohnsitz hatten, wurden diese abnormen Menschen vernichtet. Als aber der Ackersmann und Bauer (aus dem Jäger sich herausbildete) also eine fest-sitzende, Boden-gebundene Gemeinschaft entstand, wurden die abnormen Menschen betreut. Auch heute sorgt noch das Dorf für ihren Epileptiker oder Debilen, weist ihm die ihm gemäße Arbeit zu und versorgt und nährt ihn.

Mit der Entstehung der grossen Städte, vermehrte sich auch das Maß der abnormen Menschen, so dass immer größer die Zahl derer wurde, die nicht mehr der menschlichen Stadt- und Grossstadtgemeinschaft einverleibt werden konnte. Die öffentliche und private Fürsorge nahm sich dieser Menschen an und versuchte das ihre an ihnen zu wirken.

Es entstanden die grossen Bewahrungsanstalten, die es sich zur Aufgabe setzten, den Abnormen ein menschenwürdiges Dasein zu gewähren. Und weiter noch entstanden Schulen und Hilfs-

1.

Perhaps the old strategic law of 'March alone; fight united' was behind our plan. The friends' gradual exodus from Vienna began in early summer. One went to Paris; another to Prague; a small group was given permission to stay in Basle temporarily. The others fled to Milan, Zagreb, London and Zurich. It was comforting to know that nearly everyone had already left Vienna well before I could consider leaving the city. At that point my influential patients began to be helpful to me and by means of high level protection I acquired a visa for Switzerland. Initially my wife and our four small children were to move to Gnadenfrei (in Silesia) to stay with relatives until a new home could be found. We hoped that this would be possible within a few months: If there would be only one more opportunity to move freely again, our intentions could be realized. This is how vague and uncertain our plans were at that time! Everything was built on hope alone.

The torment and misery became noticeably worse in Vienna. The Party and the authorities soon began to pressurize me and I knew that I would have to act quickly if I was to escape the Gestapo's web vanishing without a trace. An Italian patient who had become a family friend the previous year, travelled from Rome by car to help arrange my departure during those last weeks. Donna Lucia de Viti de Marco was still able to accomplish certain things that were now beyond my possibilities. Undaunted and filled with courage, she confronted the petty tyrants. We left Vienna together on Sunday, August 14. My wife and children stayed behind — being 'Aryan' they were still somewhat protected. Donna Lucia took me safely across the border. It was a miraculous crossing made possible with the help of a drunken SA trooper. I had made it to Italy, escaping the murderers' clutches. I spent a few days with Donna Lucia and

Opposite: Plan for the Development of a Curative Institute in the South of Ireland sent in 1938 by Dr König to the Irish Government. *See page 157 for translation.*

her sister, Donna Etta in their country house in the Apennine Mountains. I was in a strange state of mind: tired, alone, without a tangible goal and therefore also without a sense of the way forward. Goethe once described this condition in *Wilhelm Meister:* 'The human being,' it reads, 'cannot be placed in a more dangerous position than the moment when — as a result of external difficulties — a great change takes place in his circumstances and he has not been able to prepare his feeling and thinking for this change. Then an epoch without epoch can arise, and the less that the person notices that he is not equipped for his new conditions, the greater the contradiction overshadowing his circumstances.' This 'epoch without epoch' had begun for me. As I had no means of supporting myself — at that time refugees were only allowed to take ten German marks away with them — all I could do was to watch as I was moved from place to place.

To begin with I lived for a time at Gwatt on Lake Thun where the Baroness B. took care of me — in her way, but generously. I met many interesting people, amongst others Carl Zuckmayer, the dramatist, old Baron Andrian, in his youth friend of Hofmannsthal, and Hans Müller, the writer. These people were also blind to what was happening in Central Europe. While National Socialism was certainly abhorred, at the same time they believed that the whole business would be over in a matter of months. This group was so naïve that one of them — a Count M. — had begun to write a novel describing the love between a German farmer's son and a Czech working girl. He truly believed that his novel could prevent occupation of the Sudetenland countries! I mention this example in order to characterize how lost and confused the elite were at that time.

Not long thereafter I visited Arlesheim where I was received warmly by Dr Wegman but with the greatest reserve by the workers at the clinic and at the Sonnenhof. I realized that it would be impossible to stay there for any length of time. I negotiated with the director of the Swiss Epilepsy Association in order to secure a work position in their laboratory. As I had already been developing new ideas for the treatment of epilepsy for quite some time, and empirical proof and confirmation were still needed, I thought this would be a productive use of the time given to me. Soon after their initial agreement, however, I was informed that there was no interest in my inadequately substantiated statements.

On September 20 I travelled to Paris to look for new possibilities. France appealed to me. I sensed that I would be able to work there and to bring our plans to fruition. There were not only cheaply available houses but also entire villages that had been left completely deserted. So I sent the first circular letter to the friends from Paris. While the letter offered only vague hopes, it was nevertheless positive about the possibilities for our work to develop in France. A little more than a week later the Munich 'betrayal' took place. The stance taken by both Chamberlain and particularly Daladier gave me much food for thought. Would France survive if it continued to ingratiate itself so intimately with the devil?

On my return to Switzerland I travelled to Vevey on Lake Geneva. One of my former patients from Vienna, a violinist, Bronislav Hubermann, had invited me to spend a few weeks at his home. I could find no peace there at all, however, and soon left again. It seemed to me as though a decision — a turning point — was imminent. Dr Wegman kindly arranged for me to give a lecture course within the framework of her nursing training and Dr Marti, my friend in Basle, organized a series of public lectures at the Bernoullianum. These gestures truly helped me to survive the 'epoch without epoch.' A larger number of patients came to see me and gradually I began to feel somewhat integrated with life once again. In mid-October a letter arrived from the British Consulate in Bern. I was one of fifty Austrian doctors who had been given the permission of His Majesty's Government to study medicine and work as a doctor in Britain. Was this the expected sign of destiny? I had personally never

Any communication on the subject of this letter should be addressed to:—

THE UNDER SECRETARY OF STATE,
HOME OFFICE
(ALIENS DEPARTMENT),
STANLEY HOUSE,
MARSHAM STREET
LONDON, S.W.1,

and the following number quoted:—

K 12858

NATIONAL SCHEME FOR DISABLED MEN

HOME OFFICE,
STANLEY HOUSE,
MARSHAM STREET,
LONDON, S.W.1.

18th November, 1938.

Sir,

With reference to Dr. Karl Koenig's application for permission to establish himself in medical practice in the United Kingdom, I am directed by the Secretary of State to say that he decided, subject to confirmation by the British Consul General of Dr. Koenig's suitability for medical practice in the United Kingdom, to raise no objection to his proceeding to this country with his wife and children in order to study for a British medical qualification. When he has been placed on the British Medical Register, after a period of not less than two years' study, the Secretary of State will be prepared to consider sympathetically an application for him to establish himself in medical practice in this country.

A communication was sent to the British Consul General at Zurich on the 3rd October.

I am, Sir,
Your obedient Servant,

[signature]

The Secretary,
German Jewish Aid Committee,
Woburn House,
Upper Woburn Place,
W.C.1.

Letter from the Home Office of 18 November 1938 permitting König's entry to the United Kingdom made an application to the British government. Who could be behind this?

I discussed everything with Dr Wegman and she was of the opinion that I should immediately respond to this helping hand stretched out towards me. Previously she had told me about friends living near to Aberdeen who were prepared to provide assistance to a group of refugees. She considered it vital that curative work should begin in Scotland, thereby fruitfully complementing the work that had already started in England. She also promised to give us as much help as possible. And so it came about that I travelled to Bern to collect my entry visa where I was given the assurance that all members of my family could apply for their visas at the Consulate in Breslau and would be able to join me in England at any time. The question as to who my benefactor was remained unanswered. Had the die been cast? This was on October 20, 1938, two months after we fled from Vienna.

The shoe shop of Karl König's parents

A Biographical Sketch

Peter Selg

Karl König was the first of Rudolf Steiner's great medical pupils who never actually met him but who nevertheless fully embraced the teacher's spirit and intentions in his work and endeavours. After many successful years in general medical practice, König set about building the core of his life's work which focused on children with special needs — and he achieved this amidst the ruins and destruction of the mid-twentieth century. As a baptized Jew and a Christian doctor, he salvaged a curative education movement of momentous social and religious strength from the abyss of National Socialism and the Second World War. This movement was to develop its prolific international work under the guiding star of Rudolf Steiner and anthroposophy. Throughout his life König endeavoured to develop and advance Steiner's suggestions in a methodical way and consequently he bequeathed a vast wealth of scientific work, some complete, some fragmentary in its nature.

★

Karl König was born on September 25, 1902, the only child of Jewish parents. The families of Adolf and Bertha König were respectively of Burgenland and Moravian descent and had emigrated to Vienna at the end of the nineteenth century. König's life was rooted in many generations of the rabbinic tradition through his father's family line, and hence it is significant that the family resettled in Vienna following an accident in which his religious grandfather became a paraplegic. Thus the family's move to the Central European metropolis bore the character both of 'religion' and of 'trauma and disability.' It is also essential to König's life story that his three sisters and his father's brother were murdered in Nazi concentration camps.

Two weeks prior to König's birth in Vienna, Rudolf Steiner's book, *Christianity as a Mystical Fact,* was published in Berlin. At Berlin town hall two weeks later, Rudolf Steiner spoke publicly for the first time about 'Monism and Theosophy.' Steiner reported on this event in a letter: 'I spoke for one and three quarter hours in front of ... more than 300 people, ... with their closest attention. I labour under no illusions here, but I think that most of those who were present became aware that this was something they should not allow themselves to ignore.'[1] Twenty years later the Viennese boy whose parents owned a shoe shop also gained the very same insight.

Karl König came into the world with club-feet and hence with a minor handicap. In his early years he was often transported around the city in his little cart — described by Walter Johannes Stein, a Viennese boy ten years older than him who witnessed this, as 'a king in his carriage.'

From the very beginning, Karl — known as 'Karli' — was a particularly serious and solitary child of a remarkably alert intellectuality. Following the tradition of the Talmud students he learned to think through reading and was soon able to navigate the Hebrew language with confidence. Karli helped his parents with their shoe business, he had only a few friends and apart from school he was taught by a tutor at home: 'In some things I was rather headstrong and so my attendance of primary and secondary school was not without problems.'[2]

König made his own way in the world early on in life. When he was only eleven, his parents found a picture of Christ hidden away in his wardrobe. Later, he wrote about his experience of reading the New Testament as a young boy: 'I felt I had met something that I had long been searching for and that my life would be deeply influenced by it from that point onwards.'[3]

Every morning on his way to school, Karl — this child of deeply religious Jewish roots — passed a hospital gate upon which Christ's words were written: 'In as much as you have done it unto the least of my brethren, you have done it unto me.' This almost appears as a characteristic motto of his future life — at this dawning moment, the lonely, melancholic, searching and contemplative Jewish boy comes upon a gate at a place of healing upon which the signs of Christianity were written as a 'mystical fact.'

It is also relevant that by the end of his childhood, that is, at the beginning of his teenage years, Karl König showed remarkable social conscience and was aware of poverty in the world around him. Mindful of his own good social and economic standing, during the World War years he became noticeably ashamed of his family's modest prosperity and began to give away his clothes. His mother's personal admission to a friend who had drawn her attention to the deterioration in her son's attire is moving and at the same time a powerful indication of König's character: 'It is his will and therefore we can do nothing about it.'[4] Later on many others experienced something similar in their interactions with Karl König and his intentions.

The melancholy that burdened Karl König throughout his life continued to increase during the years of the First World War without abating, so much so that his parents became deeply concerned: 'We were afraid to open the doors, wondering if we would still find him alive and well.'[5] When the war came to an end, however, the sixteen-year-old König became involved with a socialist youth group where he spoke with young workers and visited workers' colleges. He experienced this as a "step into the reality of human society."[6] It was during this time that the old Habsburg Empire in Central Europe collapsed.

In 1919 Karl König confessed to his Jewish father that he had acquired a Christian orientation and one year later he was baptized in the Catholic Church. At this same time König intensely engaged in studying problems relating to the theory of cognition, drawing on philosophical books and on his own considerations which he contemplated in depth: 'I was moved in the depths of my being by the riddle of the reality of the visible world, of the forming of ideas and imaginations, and the process of thinking, above all. For many days and nights I attempted to observe my thinking in order to find a clue to the process of acquiring knowledge.'[7] Independently from Rudolf Steiner's early writings on the theory of cognition König contemplated their key issues at a time of agnosticism; in conclusion he decided to study medicine for ethical and moral reasons and for his love of nature. His ambition was to lead 'a gracious life in God' close to nature as a medic responsible before men and all creatures alive.[8]

At the time when Karl König began his preparatory year at the University of Vienna in 1920 with extensive studies in botany, zoology and embryology the first anthroposophical course for practising doctors and medical students was held in Dornach, Switzerland. Half a year later, in autumn 1920, the Goetheanum as an independent School for Anthroposophy was opened; at the same time Dr Ita Wegman bought a property in the neighbouring village of Arlesheim to bring Rudolf Steiner's teachings to practical medical work. The first medical course in Dornach in spring 1920 had given the participants the opportunity to bridge the gap between orthodox medicine based on empirical science and the insights of anthroposophy. At the end of the course the participants drafted a declaration to raise funds for the completion of the School in Dornach ('including special institutes for each field of research') and the development of a bigger clinic; this declaration also included the following statement:

> This course has established fundamental understandings of such importance concerning the whole of the medical sciences as well as instructions for successful diagnostics, therapy and social care. Therefore a key requirement of medical work is to build a medical-scientific institute

> under expert management, as part of the Goetheanum in Dornach, in order to create a place where extensive systematic work based on anthroposophy can be carried out.[9]

At the same time in Vienna König, who was in the process of starting at university, noted in view of his medical studies: 'The ocean of materialism wants to overwhelm me. But I will stand my ground. The world and "the all" are full with God and full with angels and miracles, full of goodness and anger and full of will and intentions.'[10]

Captivated by the wonders of the organic world, Karl König studied the works of Darwin, Haeckel, Driesch, Verworn, Von Uexküll, Hertwig and others in search for the principles of life but he 'could not find either satisfactory or sufficiently extensive insights'[11] that he was looking for. Through his work as an assistant at the Institute of Embryology during his early student years did he slowly and gradually come to his own insights 'into the forces governing formation of the human embryo,'[12] and into the sphere of life. With deepest devotion he studied the formative forces working in the development of natural forms. When König discovered Goethe's writings on natural science at the beginning of the nineteen-twenties he experienced this as a 'release' which 'freed' his thinking in the same way 'in the same way that the New Testament had awakened my senses for a new dimension of existence.'[13]

With great commitment König studied morphology and the developing form of the human organism as well as the processes of metamorphososis accentuated by Goethe; at the same time he considered the connection between the formative processes in the natural world and the processes in the human mind and soul: 'Outside in nature these formative forces work in such a way that they bring all organic forms into being, while inside, in the human soul, they are the creators of our thoughts and ideas.'[14]

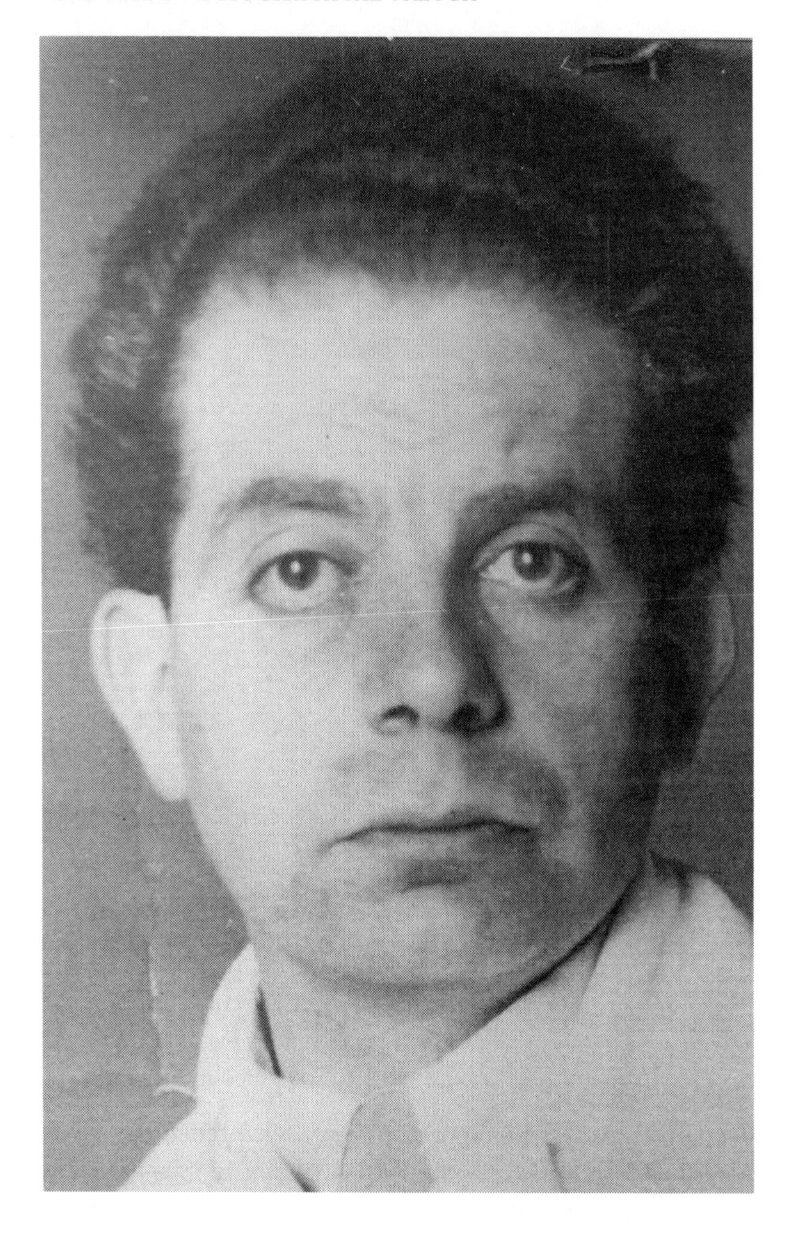

During his medical studies König was deeply disappointed with many of his teachers at university. He felt that they weren't committed to the students and their learning process and, above all, to the patient and his treatment. The Viennese Medical School was still dominated by 'therapeutic nihilism' the principle ideas of which König rejected and which was alien to König as a person. Self-reliant and on his own König made himself familiar with homeopathic therapy and began to treat patients at his parents' home. He continued to work at the Institute of Embryology where he attempted to prove the efficacy of homeopathically diluted substances by carrying out experiments with frog larvae, in which he tracked development and metamorphosis of the larvae after additions of homeopathic dilutions of silver and lead administered in increasing potency. König published his research in the *Archiv für experimentelle Medizin* and held a lively and much-debated lecture at the Vienna Biology Society.

*

In all these efforts König remained mostly alone. His diary notes of these years trace his inner search; they served as a substitute for talking to people in reflective conversations which were out of König's reach when it came to his actual concerns: 'With regard to essential questions I had the sense that I could hardly make myself understood to other people. In conversations and discussions with my few friends I continually encountered their complete incomprehension.'[15] In 1921 he noted in his diary:

> In recent days I underwent an experience hitherto unknown to me. The physical environment disappeared from around me for hours and I was able to glimpse the most inner of worlds. I understood that we are part of the whole of eternity, the universal All; and that the I *is* the universal All. In these hours I experienced my

> consciousness as far greater and more far-reaching than the stars. Time seemed to stretch out for very, very long periods. It seemed to me as if in these hours I had grasped 'thinking' for the very first time.[16]

König's remarkable entry about the experience of his thinking and of his self — in its cosmic context — can be compared to lines written by Rudolf Steiner in 1881 (at the same age as König) to a friend:

> Dear trusted friend! It was on the night of January 10 to 11 when I did not sleep for one moment. I finally lay down on my bed after working until half past midnight on a number of philosophical problems. My intention, last year, had been to establish whether Schelling's statement was true, when he says: 'We all have the secret and wonderful capacity to withdraw from transience and, above all, from everything that comes towards us from outside, into our innermost, unclothed selves and therein to behold eternity's unchanging permanence in us.' I believed then and still believe now that I then discovered in clarity that inner capacity — having already sensed it for a long time. The whole philosophy of idealism now stood before me in an essentially modified form. What is a sleepless night compared to such a discovery![17]

Without wishing to bring Steiner and König's individual spiritual experiences too hastily into parallel, this is nevertheless a moving comparison. The similarity in these experiences is as evident as is the great difference in the way in which they were communicated. Rudolf Steiner wrote to a 'dear and trusted friend' — naturally, at that time and also later he had many social connections. In contrast, Karl König was alone with his journal, and in a certain way he remained alone for most of his life despite the community life he facilitated later in Camphill.

In that same year, 1921, König came across one of Rudolf Steiner's verses at an art exhibition. The words spoke directly to König's heart and as a result of this experience he began to occupy himself intensively with Steiner's work. *Goethe's World Conception*, published in 1894, was the first of Rudolf Steiner's books that he read and that impelled him to search even further, 'because what was written there was largely already known to me.'[18] When studying Goethe König had indeed come to the same results as Rudolf Steiner in regard of the principles of life but also regarding the theory of cognition. Pleased and bemused at the same time he continued to read Steiner's writings; after a lecture on the metamorphosis of bones held at the university in Vienna by Eugen Kolisko (a Viennese doctor nine years his senior, who had become a Waldorf teacher and school doctor), König bought a copy of Steiner's *Philosophy of Freedom*. Soon after he had written this book in 1894, Rudolf Steiner said about it in a letter that it should be understood as *personal experience*.

> I do not *teach;* I am giving an account of what I have inwardly *experienced.* I relate what I have lived. Everything in my book is meant personally. Also the forms of thought. ... First of all, I wanted to show the biography of a soul striving to freedom. There is nothing to be done for those who wish to take one over cliff-edges and abysses. One must find out for oneself how to conquer them ... I went my way as best *I* could; afterwards I described *this* path. ... Philosophy really only interests me in as much as it is individual experience.[19]

The *Philosophy of Freedom* had found its way to Karl König in the fullest sense of Steiner's words, 28 years after its first publication. Again König was in full agreement, even inner accordance, the true extent of which he found almost unsettling:

> That was it! Here I could read — often in the same words — what I myself had written about the creative

DIE

PHILOSOPHIE DER FREIHEIT.

GRUNDZÜGE

EINER

MODERNEN WELTANSCHAUUNG.

VON

DR. RUDOLF STEINER.

Beobachtungs-Resultate nach naturwissenschaftlicher Methode.

BERLIN.

VERLAG VON EMIL FELBER.

1894.

Title page of Rudolf Steiner's Philosophy of Freedom

> forces in nature and human thinking! This was a deep and terrible shock for me. Had I somehow copied it all? Or was it a truth revealed to every searching thinker?[20]

Although, over the following years, Karl König was part of a group studying medical spiritual science with Norbert and Maria Glas he nevertheless remained distant from the anthroposophical movement. He did not participate in the large East-West Congress of Whitsun 1922 in Vienna that was hosted and prepared by Eugen Kolisko and which attracted thousands of people. Thus König missed the opportunity to hear Rudolf Steiner speak on numerous evenings. 'My studies, a measure of youthful egotism and also phlegma stood in my way.'[21] König missed hearing all lectures Rudolf Steiner held during the congress and also the opportunity to attend a more informal event when Steiner spoke about 'Anthroposophy as striving for a permeation of the world with Christianity' which addressed key motives in König's life. König also did not attend Steiner's lecture cycle on 'Anthroposophy and the heart-imbued intellect' which took place one and a half years later in Vienna at Michaelmas 1923. König even ignored an invitation by Norbert Glas to join a private meeting of Viennese doctors and scientists with Rudolf Steiner.

★

Then again, during the same period of time, König experienced how research in natural science and spiritual science could possibly converge. At the Institute of Embryology he engrossed himself in the study of human embryo development in its earliest stages. He had seen for himself that the amnions of the embryo develop before the embryo itself takes shape. In previous years Rudolf Steiner had referred to this phenomenon and its anthropsophical interpretation in some of his lectures which came to König's attention. Consequently König tried to show the parallel between the phases of Creation described in Genesis and the stages of early human embryo development, and also to reformulate Ernst Haeckel's biogenetic law on the basis of anthroposphy. Some years later, when König was already a member of the Anthroposophical Society and was asked for the first time to deliver a scientific lecture as part of a public anthroposophical congress, he received considerable recognition for his work on this subject. 'Members of the Anthroposophical Society began to be aware of me.'[22]

At the same time König continued to keep his self-chosen distance. He was not at all sure about the Anthroposophical Society — and he felt uneasy within it. Furthermore he felt that the bourgeois middle classes had taken over Rudolf Steiner's spiritual science, had drained it of its social-revolutionary power and had turned it into the private experience of privileged circles. This König rejected from the depth of his soul.

★

Rudolf Steiner died in Dornach on March 30, 1925, never having met Karl König in person. König later wrote: 'The news shook me to the roots of my being: I felt numb in the face of this enormous loss.'[23] Within a few months of Steiner's death, in the summer of 1925, Karl König travelled for the first time to Dornach and was profoundly impressed. In Dornach, the place where Rudolf Steiner had worked, he had a sense of belonging which related to a significant part of his self.

★

Karl König was awarded his doctorate in medicine in Vienna in the spring of 1927, and soon after began working at a small hospital in lower Austria near Klosterneuburg, an important Cistercian monastery. In his free time the young doctor sat in the library of the seminary or in the garden, gazing at the Danube below and across to the Marchfeld plain. It was there that he became 'clearly conscious' — as never before — of his Central European, Austrian identity.[24]

In autumn of the same year, 1927, Karl König gave the lecture mentioned above as part of the anthroposophical congress, and at the same time was offered post-doctoral work in embryology at the university. After a conversation with the dean of the medical faculty König refused and left the Institute for Embryology — the university had refused to allow him to include anthroposophical aspects in his lectures following his enquiry concerning this matter. Like Eugen Kolisko who also came from Vienna and from an academic family of good standing Karl König sacrificed a promising academic career in Vienna and chose anthroposophy instead. Only a few years previously, during the Christmas Foundation Meeting of 1923/24, Rudolf Steiner had said to Kurt Magerstädt: 'You can become a university professor — or you can become an anthroposophist.'[25]

After König had left Klosterneuburg he worked as an assistant doctor at a large children's hospital in Vienna. Around this time he met Ita Wegman with whom he was in correspondence since he had been accepted to the Anthroposophical Society. Ita Wegman was Rudolf Steiner's closest medical colleague, managed an anthroposophical clinic in Arlesheim and was the head of the Medical Section at the Goetheanum. Now she unexpectedly crossed König's path.

> I stood on the railway platform feeling somewhat reserved and uncomfortable. Some friends and I had been asked to welcome Ita Wegman in Vienna — her visit was because of the death of Rudolf Steiner's only sister. I had not yet met Ita Wegman and I asked myself what it meant that I would be greeting someone whom I did not know in the company of friends. At that time I was 25 and very shy, and found the company of large numbers of people difficult. After the train arrived and

> Ita Wegman had shaken everyone's hand — and I was also introduced — it was all over very quickly. I went home not knowing what all of this had meant.[26]

This first encounter at the railway station was not to be the last one. A few days later Karl König and Ita Wegman met again for a private conversation.

> As I sat opposite her I felt comfortable and inwardly free. After asking me a few questions about my life and my work, she invited me to work at her clinic in Arlesheim. I was quite surprised but also pleased at being offered the opportunity to come to the source of anthroposophical therapeutic work. I asked when she would be expecting me in Arlesheim — imagining that in any case I would complete my clinical year in Vienna — and with a smile she said that she expected me to arrive in a few weeks. I was somewhat shocked and so I resisted and defended my position, but she would not give way and it was finally agreed between us that I would start at the Arlesheim Clinic at the beginning of November. I left this meeting filled with the experience of Ita Wegman — this great personality whom I had immediately recognized.[27]

When Karl König arrived in Arlesheim at the beginning of November 1927, extensions to the Clinical Therapeutic Institute were already complete. Increasingly, Wegman's clinic had become the place for training courses for medical students and nurses. Scientific activities at the clinic and at the affiliated pharmaceutical laboratories also developed rapidly. In the previous year, 1926, Ita Wegman published the first edition of *Natura,* a journal which created the opportunity for many young anthroposophical doctors to make their therapeutic experiences and insights public; soon König, who felt 'comfortable and inwardly free' in Ita Wegman's company — as hardly ever in his life —

also belonged to this group of people. He also enjoyed the work environment at the Clinical Therapeutic Institute in Arlesheim — it was busy with activity and full of enthusiasm about starting a new era of therapy, knowledge and research in the fields of medicine, care, the art of healing and social life.

★

On the very same day that he arrived in Arlesheim, König met Mathilde Elisabeth Maasberg, a nurse from Silesia. 'Tilla' Maasberg had founded a small curative educational home in the Eulengebirge together with her sister and Albrecht Strohschein, a young remedial teacher who had been inspired by Rudolf Steiner. Tilla had come to Dr Wegman to further enhance her professional skills and receive training and instruction for a period of time; here she met Karl König.

When König arrived in Arlesheim on the tram from Basle it was Tilla Maasberg who was there, not Ita Wegman. Soon after her return, however, Ita Wegman introduced the young Viennese doctor to the Sonnenhof, a farmhouse in the village of Arlesheim where children in need of special care lived and received support. As König noted, Ita Wegman was an impulsive personality and often acted out of immediate inspirations and ideas. Now she asked Karl König if he was prepared to spend a part of his day working at the Sonnenhof. König agreed and was deeply moved by his new task. A part of his day he spent with this group of children; he experienced their special personalities and character: 'I was instantly drawn to these children and they quickly became very dear to me. And so I spent many hours with them; learning to dress and undress them, to clean them, to play with them, to calm or encourage them, and to be their friend.'[28]

As well as starting work at the Sonnenhof, König undertook further experimental research at the laboratory of Ita Wegman's Clinic, participated in artistic and curative eurythmy courses, and treated individual patients. It was only a short time later that

Karl König at the Clinical Therapeutic Institute in Arlesheim

he took the vital decision for curative education, for his lifelong commitment to the handicapped child — the child in need of special soul care. On Advent Sunday König experienced an Advent Garden for the first time.

> [The children] sat along the walls in the biggest room in the house. In the middle of the space there was a small mound made out of green moss and earth and a candle was burning on top of it. A spiral marked out with moss lead to the small mound. Every child was given an apple upon which a small candle was fixed. Advent and Christmas songs were sung and one child after another

> attempted — alone or with help — to walk through the moss spiral to reach the central mound so that they could light their own candle from the main candle. I was profoundly surprised to behold the earnestness and joy with which each child approached the task. There was the great candle! Each small candle attached to an 'apple of sin' had to be lit from this 'proclaiming' Christmas light! And suddenly I knew: Yes, this is my future task! To awaken in each one of these children their own spirit light which would lead them to their humanity.[29]

Ita Wegman had guided Karl König into the sphere of his 'future task,' yet without specifying or naming it. König's decision for curative education was taken on the First of Advent, independently from Ita Wegman and in a context whose significant meaning appealed to his heart, to the existential dimension of his destiny.

*

Shortly after his momentous Advent experience at the Sonnenhof Ita Wegman asked Karl König to hold a medical lecture at the Christmas Conference of the General Anthroposophical Society. König was startled.

> Some weeks before Christmas Ita Wegman approached me and said, 'König, I believe you should give a major lecture at the Goetheanum.'
>
> I replied, 'But Frau Doctor, I have never held a lecture before.'
>
> And she said, 'But you will be able to do it, you will be able to do it!' ... She said, 'I will accompany you to the lecture and show you the room where it will take place and also the podium where you will stand. I will sit facing you — and then everything will be fine.'

Ita Wegman

> And so, protected by her presence, everything went very well indeed.[30]

This Christmas lecture — in front of nearly a thousand people — at the Dornach Schreinerei signalled the end of König's anonymity within the Anthroposophical Society and he received many further invitations to hold lectures in Switzerland and Germany. Thus he was able to visit Lauenstein in Jena where anthroposophical curative education had its origins.

Karl König discussed with Ita Wegman the topics of his numerous lectures which were just beginning in 1928. König saw Wegman — due to her spiritual authority and her broad life experience — as his personal guardian spirit watching over his path. She was the connection between him and Rudolf Steiner and anthroposophy, at the same time she was of true 'sun energy' of which he greatly benefitted. She was the person he trusted, to whom he confided his concerns and questions. Later Karl König mentioned the 'spirit of brotherliness' which Wegman was able to extend to everyone, which he as well as many of her patients had experienced and which could even facilitate personal change. König was also absolutely convinced of Wegman as a doctor: 'she was without a doubt the best doctor I ever met.'[31]

There is every indication that Karl König could also talk to Ita Wegman about his embarrassment of having avoided Rudolf Steiner's lectures in Vienna, even Rudolf Steiner himself. Wegman had a big heart and a profound insight into human nature; such an honest confession she did not see as a problem but as an indication of an individual course of life with its own inevitabilities. Wegman herself told König about the time at the end of Rudolf Steiner's life. Decades later König said during a lecture in Föhrenbühl, Dr Wegman was not only Rudolf Steiner's doctor 'but also his carer. She accompanied him through the last months and days of his life, nursing him and caring for him. He once told her that these six months were, in fact, the fulcrum of her life.'[32]

★

Karl König also received invitations to eastern Germany to hold lectures in Breslau (now Wroclaw in Poland) and to visit Tilla Maasberg who had already returned to Silesia at the end of 1927. Her work at the small curative education home and the fact that her family was in a difficult situation didn't allow for a longer stay in Arlesheim. Now she asked Karl König for medical help for her sister, Lena, who was ill with tuberculosis.

Soon after his arrival in Gnadenfrei where the Maasberg family lived, König was deeply moved by the social-religious tradition of this Herrnhuter community and by everything he experienced of the local church, the cemetery, the landscape and in the people.

> For the first time in my life, at least that I could remember, I had stepped into true tradition. Before this I had always been independent of the past. A landscape of the Austrian mountains was my home; there I always breathed new strength into my soul; and even today I must still return again and again when I am tired and inwardly spent. It is the nature forces of the area that I draw into myself. But in considering the past as tradition, that is, as forces shaping my history — this I met for the first time in my life in Gnadenfrei. At the time I had a sense of how meaningful this moment was, but it is only today that I can truly comprehend it.[33]

Not only was König under the impression that in Gnadenfrei he encountered the evidence of a living religious tradition within a spiritual community but he also felt as if he had returned to an ancient historical place of belonging.

Tilla Maasberg and Albrecht Strohschein, curative educator and one of the Lauenstein founders, asked Karl König to join the medical work at the developing curative education institute, the more so because the provision of a property — a castle named

Pilgramshain — created the opportunity to substantially expand the project. At Arlesheim König had enjoyed a promising start full of motivation; here he was at the very centre of anthroposophical medicine and in direct contact with Ita Wegman and younger anthroposophical colleagues with great scientific and therapeutic aspirations. It was a place of crucial significance for the future of the anthroposophical art of healing, and for the past few months König had been on his way of further development, gifted with his talents and supported by Ita Wegman. Ita Wegman had brought him to Arlesheim, had encouraged him and taken him into her confidence on many occasions, obviously also counting on him and his help regarding therapy, research and teaching. For König it was difficult to abandon everything he had started in Arlesheim and to give up the close contact to Ita Wegman — yet he decided to take up the connection with Gnadenfrei and Tilla Maasberg: 'Destiny had spoken swiftly and decisively.'[34] In May 1928, after his return to Arlesheim and now twenty-five years of age, König wrote to Tilla Maasberg:

> There is only one thing I would like to say to you: In our togetherness I feel for the first time in my life that it — my life — may be redeemed. When we were together it felt like a first thawing of the innermost icy crust around my heart. The innermost Christianity in your soul and the deep spirituality of the surrounding landscape made it possible.[35]

Before taking leave of the close professional collaboration with Ita Wegman, König made an important journey together with her and a few other colleagues in the summer of 1928. They travelled to Holland to attend Willem Zeylmans van Emmichoven's opening of the Rudolf Steiner Clinic in the Hague, where König gave an address alongside Ita Wegman. The group journeyed on to London to the World Conference on Spiritual Science and its Practical Application which had been initiated by Daniel Nicol Dunlop. In July and August 1928 more than two thousand people attended the keynote lectures given by leading anthroposophists. At Ita Wegman's request Karl König spoke once again about embryology; he also attended many more lectures and met some of Rudolf Steiner's important students — for example Friedrich Rittlemeyer of the Christian Community, and a number of Waldorf School teachers from Stuttgart including Karl Schubert who originally came from Vienna. He was in charge of the curative education class of the Waldorf School since 1920 with the support of Rudolf Steiner and Eugen Kolisko and now he spoke about the education of children with learning difficulties. König, however, did not only attend lectures at the Friends House, the London Quaker centre, but he also explored the poverty-stricken quarters of this English metropolis, his heart deeply moved, even shocked by what he saw.

The World Conference in London meant a lot to Karl König; it made evident the significance of anthroposophy in terms of civilization and its social dimension which was made public by a group of highly talented people. Despite his reserve all this immediately appealed to Karl König and in a way he felt a sense of belonging.

After bidding his farewell to Ita Wegman König then travelled via Vienna to Silesia.

★

The Pilgramshain curative education home rapidly expanded after it had opened. Especially the Welfare Department for Youth in Berlin sent many socially maladjusted children and teenagers with behavioural difficulties who needed intensive support and encouragement. Apart from that a number of children were accepted for care and treatment who respresented the more specific spectrum of special needs — soon more than a hundred children and youths lived in Pilgramshain. On numerous occasions Karl König asked Ita Wegman for therapeutic advice — during her annual visits, during his short stays in Arlesheim and in letters. In April 1929, half a year after he had started in Pilgramshain and following his enquiry regarding the success rate of radiation therapy for children with Down's syndrome and the possible application of this method in Pilgramshain she wrote to him:

> This is a serious issue. Elsewhere there have been frequent initial improvements and yet it turned out later that there have been bad side effects. What is happening in these cases [of mental deficiency] can't be controlled by us so easily. The successful improvements which have been achieved by using this X-ray therapy, for instance with Down's syndrome children, have, as you describe in your letter, given these children a reasonably normal soul life. We do achieve the same effect but through the children's own individuality, whereas I feel that by using this X-ray therapy individuality is forced out by the impact and possibly something subhuman is put into these children's bodies. The same thing that happens, but in a different way, when animal glands are transplanted into human bodies. From my point of view I can never agree that at an institute which operates according to Dr Steiner's instructions such experiments are being done on issues which still need clarification. Otherwise we stray off the safe path which is destined to entice the child's spiritual being in every respect, to do everything so that the child can embrace his karma, and if this fails to do everything so that in the next incarnation a normal body can be formed. Such an X-ray intervention is not, and I know this from Dr Steiner himself, something that will get us any further.[36]

For Karl König these 'words of guidance' from Ita Wegman were of vital importance; he kept her letter for the rest of his life.

Karl König at Pilgrimshain (back row, fifth from left)

König did extensive work in Pilgramshain — and his diaries show to which degree he had already digested anthroposophical knowledge of the human being and was able to apply it to therapy. Parallel to his curative educational work in Pilgramshain and his big general practioner's practice which he established in the rooms to the right of the castle entrance König also started busy lecturing activities in Silesia, Bohemia and Berlin. He was involved in the Association for Social Support which had been founded and established by Ita Wegman and he spoke in numerous cities about social-medical issues, often together with Emil Bock, one of the founders of the Christian Community who also had married König and Tilla Maasberg.

As early as 1930 König and Bock were discussing (that is, opposing) euthanasia with social workers and welfare officers in Hamburg. At a one-week event arranged especially for social and welfare workers by Ita Wegman at the Goetheanum in Dornach in the autumn of 1930, König undertook to build links between the fields of social work and curative education. Two years later König and Bock founded a school for social work studies in Eisenach.

Like many others, also some of Rudolf Steiner's students — among them Karl König — tried to counteract with all their strength and at great personal risk the rapid dynamic of decline in the name of National Socialism by raising awareness and by truly developing one of the most threatened parts of social life — the sphere of humane curative education and social therapy. Soon König was away to lectures on nearly every evening, working tirelessly and driven by the hope that maybe just in time a wider public could be rallied. A year after he had started in Pilgramshain and after his lectures in Berlin and Hamburg he wrote to Ita Wegman:

> During my whole journey I had the strong impression that everything I have been talking about is guided by the spiritual world so that social support can establish itself within the wider context which you have always wished for. ... I hope that there will be a broad base of consent so that all those who want to practice social care on the basis of spiritual and intellectual freedom can join together.[37]

König's extensive lecture activities as well as his ever expanding practice were a considerable problem for some of the staff at the institute in Pilgramshain. König dedicated a substantial part of his energy to different issues and only partially participated in the community — even if his activities were doubtlessly of benefit for the anthroposophical movement. Countless people came to see him: 'People travelled from all over; arriving by train and car, by bus and van. Aristocracy and workers, farmers and town-dwellers all sat peaceably together in the waiting rooms.'[38] In this situation Karl König's relationship to the management of the curative education institute became increasingly complicated.

Arbeits-Abende

der „Allgemeinen Sozialen Hilfe" E. V.

Berlin W 62, Schillstr. 11a * Fernruf: B 5 Barbarossa 5182

Montag, den 29. Februar Dr. med. Grete Bockholt:
Rhythmusstörungen in der Großstadt

Montag, den 7. März Walter Hoffmann:
Aus der musikalischen Arbeit der heilpädagogischen Institute

Montag, den 14. März Dr. med. Heinrich Hardt:
Vom Einfluß des Körpers auf die geistig-seelische Entwicklung des Kindes

Montag, den 21. März Dr. med. Karl König:
Erkenntnis und Heilung psychopatischer Kinder

Beginn der Vorträge 20 Uhr

Vortragssaal: Berlin W62, Schillstr. 11a III

Freiwilliger Unkostenbeitrag erbeten.

Poster advertising evening lectures for social workers in Berlin 1932

König himself was disappointed with the institute's community and the curative education movement as a whole. He had expected more and something different regarding spiritual research and the way it was made public and also regarding anthroposophy, its significance and tasks in terms of civilization and its internal requirements. After 1933, as a Jew and anthoposophist appearing in public, König came under increasing political pressure. Yet he received only limited protection and support and at least by some he was seen as a risk to the institute and the movement which would be able to work more efficiently and safer on the quiet.[39]

After considering the situation for a while König eventually decided at the end of 1935 to leave the curative education institute together with his family and to return to Vienna. On February 26, 1936, on the eve of Rudolf Steiner's 75th birthday, König wrote a farewell letter to the institute staff and to friends of the anthroposophical curative education. He looked back on seven and a half years of work in Pilgramshain and within the anthroposophical curative-educational movement, he described both his positive and his hurtful experiences:

> Building up the institute in Pilgramshain has been part of my life's work. Looking back these years were my apprenticeship and I hope that I can now move on as a journeyman. During these years of apprenticeship I had the happiest and also most painful experiences. The rise of the remedial-pedagogical work, the big conferences in Hamburg, Berlin and London are unforgettable. All the activities with hundereds of people who had an innermost interest in our work belong to the good memories. The moments of emphatic concern when medically caring for the children are the dearest. Painful are the rather 'internal' experiences: a repeatedly failing community at the institute and between institutes, my own and my friends' complacency and the often

> blinkered view in our ranks of the outside world. And now the loss of everything that was, until a few months ago, the core of my life. But above all there is the great leadership that has brought us together, the spiritual momentum which made us start and develop all the work. There are the great breakthroughs which were shared by a community of friends and gave an immediate experience of the spiritual world. All this will stay steadfastly with us and in our community.[40]

König left Pilgramshain and went to Prague where for years he had successfully developed medical work and held medical consultations — a short time later he went to Vienna. The Bohemian landscape, the Karlstein and everything associated with it meant a lot to him; he experienced this area as a place of inner belonging and was convinced that even in the future it would be of extraordinary significance for the destiny of Central Europe:

> For many years previously the image of a 'spiritual Ostmark'* would arise within me ever and again. In difficult and also good moments in my life this image shone light on something decisive for my destiny. This 'spiritual Ostmark' encompassed Silesia, Bohemia and the eastern part of Austria. And it always seemed clear to me that I would accomplish all my work, both inner and outer, in these three countries. Here is the very pointer to — or *the* point of — my tasks: To administer so many medicines to people that the atmosphere of the whole landscape becomes clearer and more light-filled. This illumination would, I hoped, make it possible, indeed easier, for souls to descend into this landscape at the end of the century. It seems as if this landscape will also have

* König refers to the eastern border regions of the ninth-century Carolingian Empire.

> a role to play in the final battle between the forces of light and dark. And souls will be needed for this final battle, their descent made possible through the very work that we are doing.[41]

★

At the age of 34, on his own once more, König had to make a completely new start in Vienna. He had lost most of his patients as well as the curative education context in which he had worked successfully, despite various problems, for more than seven years. The curative educational community as such had been extraordinarily important to König; also his four children, who had been born during this time, had grown up there. A private or public health service practice as the focus of his work was no longer a desirable option for Karl König after he had experienced a true therapeutic community as an element of future medicine already with Ita Wegman in Arlesheim. König had continued this way of working within a community in Pilgramshain although there he had again followed his own agenda regarding his practice and his social-medical and anthroposophical lectures. Yet he needed to make a respectable effort to establish a practice in Vienna — in the city where he was born, at a low-point in his life and in difficult social and political circumstances, two years before the annexation of Austria by Adolf Hitler's National Socialist Germany. He had to provide for himself and his family, and at the same time he needed to lay the foundation for the next steps ahead. He considered starting a clinic and a children's home near Vienna, but for the time being he was occupied with the bare necessities: 'For many months ... only the essentials of daily life were available to us.'[42]

But Karl König again enjoyed therapeutical success in Vienna: the number of his patients grew from week to week. As in Pilgramshain he rapidly gained an excellent reputation as a general practitioner who was soon known across all sections of society. Anke Weihs, one of his patients who later became one of the founding members of the Camphill community, described König's charisma as a factor of his efficacy as a doctor which she had experienced in Vienna; at the end of a longer summary of their first encounter with Dr König she said with emphasis:

> In Dr König the gaze was a channel for the flow of warmth, it was in itself healing, for one felt one was seen in one's hidden truth, and always with respect and compassion.
>
> I think this first grave gaze — Dr König otherwise said little — was the initial step in healing.[43]

During a lecture at Föhrenbühl about six months before he died, Karl König said:

> The therapeutic effect that the doctor has as a personality, rather than as a prescriber of medicines could be the path to a new, let us call it 'anthroposophical medicine.' ... This means that today it is possible to envisage the doctor engaging in the therapeutic process in a new way, integrating it with his individual personality. A new anthroposophical medicine, that is to say, a 'mystery medicine,' will only become widespread when groups of people and doctors realize that a medicine can only begin to have a therapeutic effect if the patient accepts the medicine, if the doctor offers it out of his professional authority and integrity ... This is really all about the doctor once again becoming involved with the medicines and their efficacy.[44]

Alongside his daily work as a doctor Karl König held weekly lecture evenings on spiritual science for his patients at the medical practice. Soon, however, not only isolated individuals attended these lectures on anthroposophy, but a group began to form around König, finding a connection to him as a highly talented anthroposophical teacher and friend. Under his guidance they studied anthroposophy. During Advent 1937, they also gave a performance of the Oberufer Nativity play which had been rediscovered by Karl Julius Schröer and Rudolf Steiner. They were deeply moved — according to König — by the simple piety of the images and words, and felt their community generating power in the light of the event of Christ.

In addition to studying anthroposophy with König, the group started intensive considerations of the biographies of people who had died violently during the First World War — for example Franz Marc, August Macke, Bernhard von der Marwitz and Otto Braun. Karl König wrote about this work as follows: 'We sensed that these young people had attempted to prepare the ground for something we should continue.'[45] With this intention and on the basis of the individual destinies they had studied, the study group focused on aspects of reincarnation and karma as described by Rudolf Steiner.

They also began to work together on the Pedagogical Youth Course given by Rudolf Steiner in Stuttgart in 1922. Young people, mostly members of the anthroposophical students' association, had asked Rudolf Steiner for conversations after depressing experiences during the East-West Congress. Afterwards Rudolf Steiner invited the group to a rather unorthodox course, saying, 'We would like the program to arise spontaneously amongst ourselves during the course.'[46] The course that took place was of great importance for the participants. They were, as Wilhelm Rath said, 'actually conversations with the soul of youth' conducted by Rudolf Steiner — conversations of a pioneering nature.[47]

While studying the transcripts of these remarkably spontaneous lecture and considering the situation in pre-Nazi Vienna in 1937/38 it became clear to the young study group around Karl König that the focus should be on planting the seed of renewal into Central Europe's declining civilization, in continuation of the intentions of those who had died early. Already for a while the group of friends around Karl König had nurtured the wish to develop some meaningful activity together — as a group actively working out of anthroposophy into the world. Studying the Pedagogical Youth Course helped to pave this path for the friends around Karl König. A young member of the group, Peter Roth, characterized the way they approached Steiner's lecture course and the working atmosphere around Karl König.

> Our impulse took on a definite form within the landscape of Rudolf Steiner's lectures: We felt — albeit dimly perhaps — that anthroposophy is a way of life and that through it an aura develops within which the Christianity of our time can reveal itself. This meeting with anthroposophy was an extraordinary experience for us. It would not be quite accurate to say that because we met Karl König, this extraordinary man, anthroposophy became as important and decisive in our lives as it was for him. He was, without a doubt, an extraordinary person. We felt this at the first meeting and we knew that he attributed a great deal of his achievements to what anthroposophy had brought to life in him, and that a new Christianity had come to expression in him. But more important and tangible, however, was that during the one and a half years we were together with König in Vienna, anthroposophy became an individual flame in each one of us, as something made possible through him. We were able to decide to dedicate our lives to` the service of a future community, which we envisaged as a kind of vessel for a further step in Anthroposophia's incarnation. Throughout this process, which deeply affected each one of us, Karl König acted as mentor and friend. His reticence and self-restraint allowed anthroposophy to work all the more strongly through him.[48]

★

In the summer of 1937 Karl König was a guest at the Hohenfurt Monastery at Krumau (now Moravsky Krumlov in the Czech Republic) where he visited the home of the Austrian poet, Adalbert Stifter whose work he greatly admired. Later König referred to Stifter's devotion to the humble and lowly, as well as his assertion that each person is treasured by someone, as the most essential basic attitudes needed in curative education. During this particular summer, two years before the outbreak of the Second World War, Karl König also visited the Black Sea, where he engaged in a profound study of Rudolf Steiner's descriptions of the Colchis Mysteries, which also refer to the relationship between Buddha and Christianity, and the initiation of the individuality of Francis of Assisi. These study experiences deeply resonated in König's soul; they were the inner preparation for the difficult times to come, yet at the same time a call to stay on the chosen path.

German National Socialist troops marched into Vienna on March 11, 1938 — only three months after the performance of the Nativity play. On the evening of this day the study group around Karl König once again met in his practice and read the last lecture of the Pedagogical Youth Course in which Rudolf Steiner emphatically mentioned the working of the Archangel Michael in the twentieth century — as well as the social requirement to support this future working. On a day of terror which would be followed by many more, the group parted with the promise to remain faithful to the common goals.

Only one year previously, in 1937, the group had agreed to begin its common work in curative education as a deed for the future. If one considers the education, studies and career paths of these young people, however, curative educational work did not seem something they were necessarily closely connected with. Although Karl and Tilla König had some experience in this field, it was by no means a crucial factor in this decision. The focus of the group was more on forming a social community based on spirituality, a community that would contribute something essential to humanity's progress and to the realization of dignified living conditions for people. It was the 'handicapped' child, described by Rudolf Steiner as 'in need of soul-care,' which finally gave the group's intention its orientation and helped the group to find a true focal point and an inner purpose. Since his experiences in Arlesheim and Pilgramshain König saw children 'in need of soul-care' as a gift to humankind — a unique token and request to keep in mind what it means to be human. These experiences of Karl König appealed to his young friends at a time when the distortions of the concept of humankind became evident to the extreme.

But planning for the future was made difficult by the Nazi invasion. The Jewish members of the group were under threat of deportation which had started in summer 1938. With Hitler's taking power something disastrous had descended upon Austria and Central Europe preventing further development. This was nothing new to Karl König who had at the beginning 1933 been warned by Ita Wegman of the events to come. Hurriedly, and in the face of the threat, König's group drafted a 'plan for establishing a curative education institute' which was sent to the governments of Ireland and Cyprus with a request for safe passage into the country. Ireland refused, Cyprus never replied. Consequently the group — the majority of them Jewish — decided that for the time being that each member should try to flee separately. Karl König, as a Jew, but baptized Christian and prominent anthroposophist, only managed to escape from Austria very late and with the help of an influential patient. In June 1938 he could take refuge in Italy and Switzerland while Tilla and the children went to Gnadenfrei. Karl König's parents, too, luckily escaped the Nazi terror.

★

König's weeks and months in Switzerland were difficult, accompanied by personal disappointments and with no real basis for the future. It was not before early autumn that he saw light at the end of the tunnel — in France where for the past two years Ita Wegman had supported a curative education institute (run by one of König's former colleagues in Pilgramshain). Ita Wegman encouraged Karl König to go to France, too. On September 28, 1938, twice seven years to the day after Rudolf Steiner's final Michael Address to the members of the Anthroposophical Society, Karl König wrote from Paris to his circle of friends.

> It is an unusual country. I believe that it will be of great significance in the decades to come because everything seems to indicate that it will be the place for Central Europe's spiritual rebirth. There is much to be discovered here that is holy and healing. The ancient wisdom stream of Mary continues to live on and the grace emanating from it can be felt everywhere. True motherhood still resides here. Yet there is sadness in this motherliness, as in Herzeloide, when Parsifal rode away from her. He left the mother in order to find the path to the Holy Grail. Also the image of the Pieta arises time and again in the soul when one is searching for *la France.* I believe that you should take into your hearts this picture of the mother weeping over her son. It will help us on our way. Perhaps we may be able to bring comfort to this grieving mother ...
>
> Please make every effort to begin learning French. Also, if possible, I ask you to read the legend of Parsifal, particularly Wolfram von Eschenbach's version. *Notre Dame* is alive there. I will write to you soon again and at more length. Meanwhile, I ask you to answer my letter and to let me know what you have to say to my plan. I send you all my heartfelt greetings. Give our work as much thought as it needs to be born out of the pure strength of striving and thinking.
>
> In solidarity, intimately yours, Dr König.[49]

Karl König at Gwatt near Lake Thun, Switzerland, August 1938

König's letter spoke of idealistic hopes while desparately searching for a country that would welcome their project plans. König also set his hopes on 'Notre Dame' — but less than eighteen months later the German armies invaded France and were met with little resistance. What followed was the deportation of people of Jewish origin; this would have sealed the fate of König's circle of friends if they had started work in France in 1938/39. When the German troops arrived in France, however, the group was already in Scotland.

Ita Wegman had strongly advised König — after witnessing with compassion his stagnating efforts in France and in the light of an unexpected offer to emigrate to England — to go to London and from there to Aberdeen where she had well-off friends.

On December 8, 1938 Karl König arrived in London, in his thirty-seventh year, the time of the second moon node, a biographical turning point. The origin of the visa was still unclear to him — although later on he increasingly gained the impression that his friend, Eugen Kolisko, who had emigrated to London before him, had been the helping and ultimately rescuing hand.*

*

Only a few days after his arrival in London, Karl König travelled with acquaintances to Williamstown, north of Aberdeen in Scotland. Ita Wegman's friends intended to make a building available to König and his group of friends who would arrive later — an empty rectory built of granite. The building had no electricity or heating but there was running water. Following his return to London, only a few days before the Christmas celebrations of 1938, Karl König wrote to his friends.

> With a joyful heart and grateful reverence, I send you all, and all our friends, my Christmas greetings. I hope they fill you with the same joy that I am feeling. Two days ago we came much closer to realizing our goals. It seems to me that now, just before Christmas, the door has opened a crack and allowed us to glimpse the light of our future path.[50]

König followed this with an account of his experiences in Scotland, describing the landscape and his welcoming hosts. At the end of his Christmas letter he wrote with almost lyrical, hymn-like expression

> And so we have found 'our Ireland.' It sounds like a fairy tale but it is true, and I hope that a great, wholesome and

* Since König's death, Friedwart Bock has heard that it was Cecil Harwood who knew the Under-Secretary of State at the Home Office who arranged for the visa. It may have been at Eugen Kolisko's request.

> beautiful community can now be established. It appears to me to be of decisive significance for our efforts that this all has fallen into place at Christmas time. That we have found the good 'innkeepers,' that they want us, that all of our endeavours may be directed towards this initiative; that in the work of our hands, through the will of our hearts and the light of our thinking — but always in the community of our deeds — the cosmic Word can be revealed.[51]

The Oberufer Christmas plays that the group had staged, and the Foundation Stone Meditation given by Rudolf Steiner at the Christmas Foundation Meeting of 1923/24 resounded through König's Christmas letter in the same way as the final words of the Pedagogical Youth Course: 'The most important thing will be that we find ourselves within our hearts. Then the spiritual, the Michaelic, will flow into our hearts.'[52]

Despite the glimmer of hope and the optimism that König had expressed in his letters to his friends, in London König experienced difficult hours and days.

> Now I sat there, torn away from my work, and I experienced myself as shipwrecked and cast up on a lonely, unknown island. My candle flickered and cast strange shadows on the wall. I had left Europe behind me — because here was not Europe anymore; it was already a part of the western world. I could not speak the language and the people seemed strange to me. Their way of life was different from what I was accustomed to, and I knew little of their history. I came from another environment entirely and had other customs, other points of view. Some of these foreigners were friendly towards me but others, whose help I counted on, showed only as much interest as good manners required. Thus I was alone and had to fend for myself. Would I have the strength for yet another new beginning?[53]

These were Karl König's questions and reflections during the Christmas Night of 1938. But during this night, and through reflecting on the Bible he also found his inner path of destiny again. In his diary he commented:

> Already I understood more about the task that lay ahead of me. Austria was overrun by men who had betrayed the innermost essence of Europe's destiny. They had turned it into a stronghold of nationalists where only the laws of power and violence held sway. Europe was still preening itself in vain glory and was already on the way to becoming a battlefield. Could we not take up a part of Europe's true destiny and transform it into a seed, so that something of its original mission could be rescued? A part of its humanity, inner freedom, love of peace and its dignity? If this were possible, surely we had a reason to live and work again. Could we not try to establish something of this vanishing Europe? To realize this through deeds, not words? To serve and not rule, to help not force, to love and not hurt. That will be our task. Such thoughts passed through my mind, and with time I was able to understand them better. After weeks of suffering and distress they arose before me, to clarify the riddle of my existence.[54]

★

König's conversations with Eugen Kolisko, his medical colleague and friend from Vienna, were a great support to him around this time, helping him to understand the riddle of his own existence, the broader trajectory of his individuality and its path of destiny. Kolisko, something of a lone wolf, had emigrated to London in 1936, distressed and deeply hurt by the clashes within the Anthroposophical Society, which — as also in the case of König — resulted in his expulsion in 1935. The conversations with Karl König mostly focused on topics of historical interest — particularly the seventeenth century: Bohemia, Wallenstein and the Rosicrucians. Kolisko's vast knowledge of history were of significant help for König. At the same time König was immediately aware of Kolisko's own situation after Kolisko's plans to establish a major school of spiritual science in London had largely failed. Karl König had already previously recognized Eugen Kolisko's remarkable abilities and also his sensitive constitution. König's impression was that the curative education community forming at the Scottish rectory could provide significant protection for Kolisko. At the same time König was hoping for Kolisko's spiritual support for his momentuous endeavour.

König's wife and children reached London on the penultimate day of 1938 and the other members of the group arrived in the early months of the following year, amongst them Alix Roth who came from Zagreb and Thomas Weihs whose ship was the last to reach London before the outbreak of war. At the end of March, that is to say, the beginning of April 1939, the group moved into Kirkton House, the rectory.

The south window of the rectory looked out onto the Scottish Highlands and the Bennachie, a legendary double-peaked mountain. On the first night of his arrival Karl König had a remarkable dream.

> I saw a great ship land on the peak of the Bennachie — I knew it was Noah's Ark. It dropped anchor between the two mountain tops. The doors of the ship's hull opened and a huge crowd of people — men, women and children, small and tall, old and young — streamed out of the belly of the ark. They moved in great throngs from the mountain peaks down into the valley and began to inhabit the land. Confused and astonished I woke up. Was that a sign of what was to come?[55]

At the end of the first week at the old rectory the group experienced an eclipse of the sun which spread twilight over the

The early group at Kirkton House in 1939

countryside — this in a year that was marked by what was surely the most horrific war in Central European history. A war that sanctioned the systematic murder of millions of Jewish people — people like the majority of Karl König's group. The small company that had fled to Scotland found themselves in an extraordinarily difficult emotional situation. A young woman in the group, Anke Weihs, wrote later:

> Our own little bit of consciousness appeared to be like a candle flame flickering in a storm. From what source should we find the strength to kindle our will and do something together that had no name and no visible form, but which, it seemed to have been agreed, would demand the dedication of our whole existence, whether we liked it or not? It would be wrong to think that we had a close bond as a group and that we could rationally

> find our way to a common path — or even plan one. Rather we experienced a kind of spiritual vortex that threw us to and fro, cut us off from the few developing threads present in our lives, and, at times, led us into our own darkness as the outside world itself began to darken.[56]

And so, during an era that was now dominated by war and distinctly marked by deeds of 'extermination of unworthy lives,' this group embarked upon a humane path.

Only a few weeks later, at the beginning of May 1939, Karl König and his friends took the first two special needs children into their care. Soon after, in a ceremony on Whitmonday, they opened the former church rectory fir its new purpose. In his celebration address König focused on the 'Christianizing' movements in Europe, indicating that during the course of the twentieth century Christianity must be brought back to the Scottish landscape of the Hibernian mysteries in a different form, and that this should be accomplished through anthroposophy.

> We should not see ourselves as missionaries, but instead we should attempt to bring about an encounter between the British spirit and the Central European spirit — an encounter between all that is dreamed and thought in the German language and all that the British person can accomplish through deeds. We should promise each other that we will not create a Central European island here but that we will attempt, as best we can, to do everything for the benefit of this country. Let us strive to do this, knowing however that if we are unable to accomplish it, others will be able to. But let us try — and perhaps the spirit will also permit us to make a contribution.[57]

The address quoted here concluded with a reading of the Foundation Stone Meditation given by Rudolf Steiner.

Karl König was often away in England when the community was first being established. In addition to continuing his education at Aberdeen University, he had medical consultations together with Eugen Kolisko in London and held lectures in large cities such as Birmingham, Manchester and Edinburgh. By developing and broadening the basis of his lecturing activities and medical work, König was in the early stages of repeating the Pilgramshain pattern of events. But this time, the group — his friends — asked him to return to home base. König himself also realized that his presence was indispensable for the success of community's endeavour and he reduced his range of activity in order to support the Kirkton House project.

The community's study material during this period reveals how König wanted to support their work spiritually. They studied Rudolf Steiner's Curative Education Course, Christian Rosenkreutz's *Chymical Wedding* and Steiner's lecture cycles on Christology. The group considered the 'new anthroposophical curative education' to be part of the creative stream of esoteric Christianity — that was its spiritual source, its task and purpose in the middle of the twentieth century. This was the substance through which König and his friends wanted to develop their work — each of them set about 'to bring their personal destiny to bear on the developing work.'[58] There were considerable problems at the start, as König commented:

> Most of the group had been students until then and they were used to living in a rather casual way. Hardly any of them knew how to use a broom, make beds, clean rooms or do the washing. Cooking also had to be learned and so they had to undergo a tough school of self-education. Spade and shovel, hoe and rake — all were unknown tools, but the garden work demanded their use.[59]

Tilla König who had great curative educational and domestic skills instructed the young people; apart from that they were free to approach Karl König with all their questions regarding daily life and their bigger concerns in the sense of learning within a community. In the Scottish rectory family groups were formed together with the children whose days and lives were shared by their adult carers — in light and in darkness. Looking back on this, König later wrote: 'For many of us it was a revelation how "normal" children with special needs are. Day by day we discovered completely new facets of curative education.'[60]

★

At the end of November 1939, while Kirkton House was still being established, Eugen Kolisko died suddenly while alone on a suburban London train. Karl König first heard the news of his friend's death a few days later. However, immediately after Kolisko's death, König experienced an enhanced state of consciousness: 'It appeared to me as if supersensible impressions merged with daily experiences and it was not easy to distinguish the boundaries between this side and the other side with any accuracy.' Fourteen years later Karl König explained:

> I mention this because since then, and over many years, Eugen Kolisko has often been at my side. For a long time he accompanied me as my mentor, *aide memoire* and brother. I know that many of the events that followed his passing across the threshold could only have been brought to fruition with his involvement and counsel.[61]

König included Kolisko in the wider circle of friends of Kirkton House and felt strongly committed to Kolisko himself and to his destiny. This relationship lasted beyond Kolisko's death and, according to König, was an integral part of the conditions in which the community developed. In Vienna, after studying the early death of people who had been of cultural significance in the time before the First World War, König and his friends had consciously decided to continue these intentions on

Eugen Kolisko

earth. In Kolisko König now had a close friend in the spiritual world and experienced his help and support.

At the time of Eugen Kolisko's death, the Second World War had already begun. In far-off Scotland, König and his group were isolated, alone and removed from the events of Central Europe. The day after Kolisko's death, and therefore during the period of 'enhanced consciousness' described above, Karl König noted several remarkable thoughts in his journal regarding the wartime situation.

> In the midst of war, in the rush of attack and counter-attack; in the fear of annihilation and blindness of hate, amongst this death and destruction — the name of Rudolf Steiner should not be forgotten. Today everyone in this country knows that this is transforming the innermost nature of each individual. Each person who

> survives this war will emerge as one who has been baptized. But the kind of baptism each will receive will depend solely upon themselves — that is, whether their baptism leads to the heights or the depths. Today everyone also knows that this war is the first to be led by more than human will alone: machines are stronger than human will and today it is machines that lead people into battle. A human being may choose whether to be baptized by heaven or by machines. The machine was created because science failed to remember its mission. Science failed to remember its mission because human beings involved in its inauguration were no longer aware of their own inner core and being. Charles Darwin's *On the Origin of Species by Means of Natural Selection,* which saw the light of day in 1859, originated in this country. Since then the ideas in this book have come home to roost as the evil power of nationalism. Darwin established a theory of natural selection, the fruits of which now manifest as political nationalism. Thus science has two faces. The machine; and the political delusion of racial distinctions. If we are able to recognize this, then Rudolf Steiner's words, spoken on April 24, 1922 in London, become prophetic: 'Our science is advanced but it is not yet Christianized. We talk about culture, yet no one can find a reason to Christianize science. This must happen, however. Science must be Christianized — otherwise everything in the cosmos that humanity needs will be lost.'[62]

With the start of the Second World War, Karl König and his friends became 'enemy aliens' in Britain but it was nevertheless possible for their curative educational work to progress. The group also continued to nurture and develop their spiritual science studies, which were still anchored in a Central European impulse. The group performed the Nativity play at Christmas

1939 and studied Rudolf Steiner's Christology lectures on *The Fifth Gospel* during the Holy Nights that year.

At the beginning of 1940 König and his friends found the neighbouring Camphill estate. In Central Europe, in contrast, the Nazi forces spread their destruction even further afield and by spring 1940 they occupied Denmark and Norway. As the war escalated and broadened across Central Europe, England and Scotland were also under direct threat. Karl König experienced these events intensely. On April 10 he noted in his journal:

> Everything inside me seems paralysed; feelings and thoughts constantly revolve around the great battle in Norway. I sensed the dying, the sinking ships, the aeroplanes crashing and the angels searching out their people amongst all this distress.[63]

On Whitmonday 1940, all the male members of the small anthroposophical community were arrested and transported to the Isle of Man via Liverpool. Thus their work for the curative education initiative was disrupted, their personal fate was uncertain and therefore a factor in the community's hardship. Despite all this the friends around König continued their spiritual studies during their imternment, for example studying the lives and destinies of John the Baptist and Lazarus. During the night of August 29 to 30 Karl König had spiritual experiences that were significant and influential for his life and also for the curative education community. He dreamt of 'partaking in a meal in the sphere of spirit.' Only many years later did he tell his friends about this dream.

> I sat to the right of that personality who, in an earlier life, had founded the Herrnhuter brotherhood: Count Zinzendorf. We had a conversation in which he was the teacher and I was the pupil. In the course of the conversation he suggested to me that each Saturday evening people should gather to take a meal together and

> to read the Bible; and that we should attempt to understand the texts with the help of Rudolf Steiner's spiritual science. Certain circumstances enabled me to remember this experience.[64]

★

Meanwhile, the absence of their menfolk notwithstanding, Tilla König and the other female co-workers at Kirkton House decided to undertake the planned move to Camphill estate with twelve children. They succeeded in this task, although not without great hardship and the need to summon all their physical and emotional strength. Karl König was the first to be freed from detention on the Isle of Man. He returned to Scotland and reached Camphill only a few days after the Michaelmas festival. There he immediately set about his work, also regarding practical tasks. He described his activities in a letter to his friends who were still in detention. On October 24, four weeks after his release, he wrote about the situation in Camphill estate:

> Day after day I try to include you in my life and in all the work that is done here. The main work is now in the garden and outside in general. I am now mostly gardener, farm labourer and servant. Most of all I have tidied away the dung heaps which had still been on the estate in abundance since Mr Gill's times; together with the children I have collected a lot of wood and prepared it for the winter. Then there are many beds in the garden which need to be dug up and even cleared because much had been neglected for years. I have taken out many trees and shrubs which were old and useless, I have fixed the tools to some extent and I have done a few things in the house.
>
> The central heating is now up and running, the

> basement is tidy, the coal and anthracite are sorted and ready for use. Today the stairs and the rugs in the corridors have been put in and yesterday the linoleum in the cottage has been laid. It is already looking very nice here. Please tell Peter [Roth] that I have sorted his books and that they are waiting for him here.
>
> On Monday we have harvested the potatoes and brought them all in. At 4 AM at the break of dawn the farmer's horses were harnessed to the plough, steaming in the hazy mist, and all of us were out with the children and furrow by furrow collected the potatoes. The upper field yielded quite a good crop, the lower field almost none at all. This field needs to be completely dug up and thoroughly manured for the next year.[65]

Apart from this, König was involved in the release of his co-workers from the Isle of Man, speaking to the authorities, submitting certificates and giving his friends hope ('Please remain calm in this respect'). Soon König's efforts proved to be successful — and he had also taken up his anthroposophical lecturing on a larger scale by the end of October 1940; these lectures gave Camphill's intentions and goals publicity in the area. His letter continues:

> Three or four children are due to arrive soon. At present I am in negotiations about this. Yesterday evening I have started the lectures in Heathcot which is well attended. From now I will lecture there every Wednesday on the fixed stars and the planets and their connection to people. Starting at the beginning of December I will speak every second Sunday afternoon in Silhodley's House in Aberdeen about anthroposophical study of the human being. If I get permission from the authorities I will hold the mission week which has been long planned together with George Macleod in Edinburgh from

November 4 to 8, and I will speak once or twice a day to fifty to sixty students about 'Science and the Gospels.' On the 17th and 18th I am invitied to Glasgow to speak to ministers about 'New Understanding of the Gospels.'

So you see that quite a few things have already happened here und hopefully it will be more from now on.

But again and again while being busy at work I need to think that you are still staying in House No. 6, in those cold rooms, in that meaningless situation, and this is hard to bear.[66]

★

After the men were back, under a united effort of all friends, Camphill grew slowly but steadily. This place of which the community became increasingly convinced that it represented an ancient Templar site became the source of a development which König had hoped for and aspired to already for a long time. The 'Ark of Bennachie' had landed, the life that was saved stepped onto the earth again in the form of those being cared for as well as the carers themselves. At Whitsun 1941 König organised a well-attended educational conference for doctors, teachers, social workers and parents of children with special needs. He chose the title: 'Whitsun and the Education of the Child.'

As Camphill grew, so did the problems. Many very ill children found their way to the community and so the first children also died there. Karl König wanted to expand the medical provision by establishing a hospital and a training facility. However, many of his innovative medical intentions were ultimately unsuccessful because of the constraining circumstances of the time. In autumn 1942 he confided in his journal that he was increasingly becoming aware of 'how little we know about these children and how poorly we understand them.'

And still the war raged on. König likened the curative

education community to a Noah's Ark in the midst of a flood of destruction. He also saw this ark in the image of the first Goetheanum, the latter, for him, being the first 'spiritual ark' in twentieth century Central European history. Alfred Heidenreich, a Christian Community priest who had been ill and spent two months convalescing in the vicinity of the Camphill estate, had many intense conversations with König during this time. Later he recalled:

> König expounded his vision of the future. Deep and genuine, constructive and understanding as his devotion was to 'children in needs of special care,' he explained that his curative work was not entirely an end in itself but also a means to establish residential communities, in the spirit of Rudolf Steiner's teaching. One day they might become islands in which the life of the spirit can survive, when wave after wave of catastrophes will engulf humanity towards the end of the century. He thought that these 'backward' children had a mission to bring people together in communities even as they had a mission to awaken special love and compassion in their parents and other members of their families.[67]

This vision and insight motivated Karl König's endeavours to strengthen the spiritual basis of Camphill, not least of all through a close connection with the sacramental realm of the Christian Community — which was also to have a protective function for the curative education community. As far as König was concerned, Camphill's spiritually-motivated social processes were *also* an endeavour to counterbalance the social collapse of the Anthroposophical Society following Rudolf Steiner's death. König himself had experienced 'exile' and 'expulsion' in a number of ways — as a baptized Jew he had to flee from the Nazis; as an anthroposophist, he had been unwelcome and at risk, and the Anthroposophical Society had cancelled his membership. Karl König experienced the breakup of the Anthropsophical Society, founded at the Christmas Conference in 1923/24 with its admirable constitution and intentions of working into civilization, as a huge affliction and fault with continuing ramifications. The Camphill community almost assumed the character of closed 'order' in its founding years. This was supposed to stimulate a healing process in the hardship of the time and also in regard of the Anthroposophical Society which in König's view had been destined to pave the path for Christianity into science, art and religion in modern life.

> Social forms must be found to replace what has been lost through the breakdown of the Anthroposophical Society. This breakdown has happened because the Christ impulse has not been able to permeate society. Intellectual arrogance, a lack of faith and human politics have all caused the collapse of Rudolf Steiner's great social attempt.[68]

For König this effort represented the focus of his working life, the effort to help the 'revelation of the impulse of Christ' to take effect in social life.

★

In the middle of the war years, on March 4, 1943, Ita Wegman died at the age of 67 at her wooden house in Arlesheim. The news upset Karl König in every fibre of his being.

> Now this good and great woman has gone into the spiritual world. Perhaps Rudolf Steiner's best friend. The friend who cared for him day and night during his illness, the central figure in the new medicine, the new curative education. Doctor, helper, advisor for many, many people. The helper and motherly friend is no more. For me, it is as if a living nerve has been severed. I

> can hardly believe I will never again see her here on the earth. How empty it is around me suddenly.[69]

König and Ita Wegman had been writing to each other for two decades and even during the war years they had kept up their correspondence. What Ita Wegman really meant to him Karl König only seldom expressed; but during the last years of his life, in his lectures, König spoke in outline about Ita Wegman and his encounter with her, such as in the lectures at Newton Dee in Scotland in March 1960 and at Föhrenbühl in 1965. In Scotland he spoke of her death in the following way:

> For a queen, such as she was, she was profoundly alone when she died, accompanied by only a few people. Because of the war, her true friends in Germany, Holland, America and England could not be with her. And so she was completely isolated. Yet ... she was surrounded by many from the other side of the threshold and was received into the light of the Spirit Sun.[70]

According to Karl König, Ita Wegman — despite her impulsive temperament — carried the new Staff of Mercury, 'the sign of a healing peace.'[71] Her image and being accompanied him all his life.

After March 4, 1943 the portraits of Ita Wegman and Kaspar Hauser were put up next to each other on König's desk. In his 'Christmas Story,' written after the war, in which he vividly described his encounters with the souls of children who had died at Camphill, and with Kaspar Hauser the following quote can be found: 'I remembered clearly that the figure of Kaspar Hauser had always been close to my heart and I knew that his being is deeply connected to the work we are doing.'[72]

*

In 1948 König wrote in an essay.

> We now care for and educate 180 children, and if we had more space we could accommodate double the number without difficulty. The children hail from Scotland, England and the colonies — from South Africa, India, Kenya, Ceylon — so that a large group from far and wide, bound by destiny, has come together here. The teachers and nurses doctors and helpers, more than sixty in number, form another branch of this network of destiny. They come from Scotland, England, Ireland, Austria and Germany, from Bohemia, Holland, from Switzerland and Sweden. Together, in this special, sacred land, we are attempting to create an environment that is appropriate for these children with special needs. They learn to work in the garden, to plough the fields, to sow seeds, to weave and spin in the workshops, to cut wood and to carve it. In the kitchens they learn to cook and in their homes they must learn to do normal housework. They learn to sing and make music, to do eurythmy, to play the lyre. But many must first learn to listen, to speak, to walk, to think. But the co-workers are aware that the children can only learn when they, the teachers, are prepared to educate themselves; therefore, in a truly social community we learn to live with each other and fruitfully integrate our personality into the larger social context. Self-education is only possible when all members of the community share a common ideal.
>
> For that reason the training here at Camphill focuses on the image of the human being; the star we are aspiring to reach is the 'human image' in its physical, soul and spiritual form. We believe that if we are able to light up the true image of a human being in our hearts, we help all those children in whom this human image reveals itself in a distorted or deformed way. So we

> inwardly uphold what can be of constant support and healing to the children. They not only need appropriate education and support, not only the necessary medicines, not only artistic activity and the possibility to do work that is useful to the world — these children need a community of educators and nurses, doctors and helpers who inwardly uphold what the children lack: the true image of the human being.
>
> Through this practice, therapeutic education — in the way that it is being attempted here — will become a crucial social issue, as is already becoming a reality in Scotland. 'Because the social question is essentially an education question, and the education question is essentially a medical question — but only for the kind of medicine that has been made fruitful by spiritual science.' These words, spoken by Rudolf Steiner on April 7, 1920 at the Goetheanum, show that questions of medicine, education and the social life form a unity which can first be realized in caring for children who are outcasts from society. They bear the future within themselves.[73]

As far as the more strictly medical aspects of curative education are concerned, after the war König established a number of structures and processes at Camphill which broke new ground in therapeutic work. He introduced — and also initially directed and ran — the weekly, in-depth child clinics during which the life and progress of an individual child was to be reflected in depth, and which was attended by everyone who was in contact with the child. These child clinics should, according to König, focus on a profound biographical phenomenology, 'to reflect an individual's true being.'[74]

Looking back on König's work in this regard, Hans Müller-Wiedemann later wrote:

> Those involved in the child clinics in these early years experienced these to be at the heart of König's mission to

> realize a 'mystery' medicine. Through the process of observing and seeking to fully understand phenomena in a child's biography, König's 'imaginative eye' frequently accessed the deeper aspects of a child's destiny. It was from this dimension of experience that he offered indications for the child's continuing therapy and education.[75]

König also introduced the morning clinics which took place in the Camphill houses where the children lived. Accompanied by the community's doctors, nurses and teachers, König saw children individually at these sessions. Like much else that König accomplished in his life, these consultations were of an exemplary quality in medical, ethical and social respect. They were didactical lessons to the benefit of everyone present and they demonstrated the community's intentions: 'He was fully present at these meetings; it was as though his wise kindness embraced each child whom he saw with a mantle of love. These discussions always resulted in new therapeutic indications and medical prescriptions.'[76]

Furthermore, König founded a curative education school in the autumn of 1947 which was named after John the Evangelist and officially opened by Karl Schubert on St John's day in 1948. From 1951 onwards both the special needs children and the co-workers' children received their schooling there. At the end of the 1940s König inaugurated a curative education seminar that provided anthroposophically-based education and further training for co-workers. Through the work of observing, seeking to understand and supporting children with special needs — indeed, human beings in general — a new kind of humanitarianism was to be learned and developed at Camphill, and from there, to spread out into human culture generally.

König's own medical work was also constantly at the heart of his endeavours: He organized conferences, published a multitude of scientific papers and broke new ground in a number of different therapeutic areas. In doing so König tried to keep up with the current scientific and clinical knowledge, at least within the fields relevant for curative education. He regarded other therapeutic approaches without prejudice — also those outside of anthroposophical medicine — and was frequently enthused and fascinated when he saw that progress was being made. We read of one such an example in a letter.

> I wanted to write only a few words to you because I believe I saw something yesterday that is completely unprecedented and revolutionary in the treatment of spastic and athetotic children. You know that a few weeks ago I heard about a Mrs Bobath who has discovered a new method of movement therapy. Yesterday I saw her and two children whom she is treating ... Because Mrs Bobath's approach does not call on the consciousness of the child, those children with the most severe of special needs can also be treated. I believe this woman has made an 'Archimedian' discovery: she brings the children into an embryo-like position and from there leads them through the infant movements back to normal movement patterns of a

> small child. One or two of us must go to London as soon as possible to learn about this. Then we will be able to truly be of help.[77]

To Karl König's great regret he often lacked the time and tranquillity in his daily life that would enable him to work more thoroughly with his insights and knowledge and develop these into a 'greater whole' — that is, a more complete body of work. However, already during the Second World War he engaged intensively with the problems and riddles of the Down's syndrome children and also gave lectures on this subject. He recorded the following in his journal: 'Much can be said about the embryological characteristics of Down's syndrome; to me it appears more important to grasp the "idea" underlying the Down's syndrome children and then present this clearly to the world.'[78] Karl König only managed to accomplish this in an extraordinary book many years later, following a near-fatal illness — and at the point when he had finally begun to retire from his numerous Camphill responsibilities.

★

In June 1953 Karl König wrote in his journal:

> In the morning I compiled a list of all co-workers both here and in the south, and I realize there are over two hundred. I am astonished at these numbers; I would never have thought it. Somewhere in myself I feel rather nervous about having responsibility for so many people.[79]

In the early years after the Second World War, Karl König was unquestionably the central figure in the Camphill community — he was responsible for the success of the whole initiative and, at the same time, he was a fraternal member of it. After 1949 his bedroom and his study — as well as his library and all his scientific publications — were on the first floor of Camphill House

where he could be in the closest possible proximity to the lives of the youngest and most difficult children in the community's care. In addition to the wealth of medical and social leadership responsibilities, the burden of administration also fell on the shoulders of this small man from Vienna.

Alongside all these tasks which König took on every day, the small and the great — including overall medical responsibility and development of the community's social structure and its cultural and religious dimensions — he represented the spiritual authority and was his colleagues' spiritual teacher. In additon he was a much sought-after partner for conversations regarding crucial personal situations in the lives and destinies of the community members, situations which never ceased to arise. Hans Müller-Wiedemann described the special sphere when encountering Karl König.

> If one sat opposite König, one could, at first, have the fleeting impression of a character out of the late nineteenth century: The correct, always considered, slow movements; the made-to-measure clothing — suit and waistcoat, a watch chain swinging from one of the

side pockets (every now and then he took the watch out of the pocket and looked at it with his head tilted slightly sideways); the prevailing order in his study. If he entered into conversation, however, this impression did not last very long and was as if extinguished by the unconditional presence of his whole being. One was aware of a kind of particularly enlivened and 'fullness' of presence when he spoke or listened attentively. It was perhaps largely through sensing this presence that one felt fully part of the conversation; that it became possible to leave all superficialities aside when speaking. König had a highly developed ability to sense the essential, and with this sense he also discovered the potential that was still slumbering in a person. He could comfort, not always through advice or explanation alone, but also through something that radiated from his being and became apparent in the very wrinkles of his facial expression and his gaze; something that pointed to a deeper aspect not usually present in human beings. If one sat opposite him in conversation, one had the impression of extreme concentration merged with a mood of completely open expectancy, as if one was the first conversation partner ever — and the only one. One noticed that he was prepared — and I doubt that he ever held a private conversation without due inner preparation. While many have experienced the compassion of his conversation, many have also experienced the unsettling — bordering on explosive — anger that could erupt from him like a volcano. This tended to happen when one had not taken oneself seriously enough, when one exercised less self knowledge than one was actually capable of, or when one blamed someone else for one's own misfortune.[80]

*

The year 1953 was difficult for the 51-year-old König. As Hans Müller-Wiedemann gleaned from his diaries and numerous other documents, this year in Karl König's life marked the beginning of his withdrawal from further developing the Camphill community which increasingly found its own way without König's direction and guidance. König noted in his journal:

> It becomes apparent to me that as far as the Community is concerned we are now in the year 1923. At that time the old Goetheanum had burnt down, just as now the old Community is dissolving, and the new will take shape in the same way that the Christmas Foundation Meeting came into being. This corresponds to the time of the ten days between Ascension and Whitsun, when the disciples were completely abandoned. This is how it is now — and it must be endured.[81]

Camphill had long since outgrown the first stages brought about by karma and destiny, a process that König experienced and suffered intensely, although one that he himself had ultimately made possible. In 1953 he intensified his efforts to evaluate his own life, even reviewing the old case-histories from his Pilgramshain medical practice. He noted in this connection:

> Patient after patient comes before my mind's eye, and I have to think how strange my life has been until now; how many people have felt drawn towards me and how, wherever I have found myself, this flow has never ceased. Why it was like this, I cannot say.[82]

König was dissatisfied with fact that many of his scientific studies were rather fragmental and had been left at the stage of a first approach, but at the same time he also saw the obvious positive moments and motives in his life and destiny. In particular he recollected the deep spiritual experiences with Count Zinzendorf on the Isle of Man which had ultimately led to the introduction of the Bible Evening — a vital element of the spiritual community: 'I turn to what happened on August 29, 1940 and am deeply affected by the miraculous world of these words.'[83] On August 30, 1953 König, for the first time, told his friends in Camphill about the spiritual background to the Bible Evenings which he had initiated during the war, to which there had been some resistance but for which he had provided little justification at the time.

König's encounters and relationship with Eugen Kolisko and Ita Wegman which were of crucial significance for his destiny also were of major importance for his biographical reflections. In 1953 König wrote his extensive obituary for Kolisko.[84] In respect of Ita Wegman he recollected Ephesus and the Logos mysteries of this ancient lustration site of which Rudolf Steiner had spoken in such a memorable way.

Considering his own karma beginning with the ancient spiritual community in Ephesus, he wrote:

> I went to Palestine, the others did not. Arabia followed, then the post-medieval world of the seventeenth century which was connected with the Bohemian brotherhood, and only now all these threads have come together again. While the others went through the Orders (Dominican), I did not.[85]

According to this König found that his own destiny followed a developmental momentum different to that of his anthroposophical friends, a finding which explained his actual exceptional position and situation. This lack of belonging — frequently blended with strong experiences of community — was still the cause for König's regret. In his view, his development was destined by incarnations in Palestine and Arabia, he experienced his proximity to the Judeo-Christian events at the turning point of time, and to the scientific developments in the region of Gondishapur, as well as to events in Bohemia. According to König all of this separated him from his spiritual companions, its effects lasting into the present time and shaping his life in the twentieth century, 'and only now all these threads have come together again.'

The year 1953 was also that of the first great journey to Ireland, of his deepening encounter with Celtic Christianity and the landscape of the 'holy isle.' Here König created the conditions for Camphill to be established, 15 years after the Irish government had rejected the group's application. At Christmas time of the same year König spoke in Camphill about Gilgamesh and Eabani and about the Foundation Stone Meditation from 1923 and the laying of the foundation stone of the first Goetheanum in 1913 which had also been accompanied by mantras and during which Rudolf Steiner had said the 'Reversed Lord's Prayer' from the *Fifth Gospel* for the first time, 'evil holds sway.' The year ended with feelings of depression and utter failure, feelings from which König could only extricate himself through inner spiritual work: 'At the turn of the year I am alone reading recollections of the Goetheanum fire and speaking the words of the Foundation Stone.'[86]

One year later, at the end of 1954, Karl König developed a serious heart condition. Confined to his bed, he was forced to wthdraw from everything else and came close to dying.

In May 1955, in the days of his slow convalescence, König wrote to Eberhard Schickler, a friend and medical colleague in Germany whom he had known previously from their work together at Ita Wegman's clinic and with whom he still had a loyal connection.

> For some days now it appears that strength and confidence have begun to return again. So I have begun to sit at my desk for a few hours each day and am now able to view life from the vertical and not only from the horizontal. Everything looks quite different, of course, and it takes a lot of courage to want to learn that again. I could now write a whole book about the influence of the

> patient on illness and vice versa, for as a doctor it is of the greatest interest when you become ill yourself: you can observe yourself, taking direct note of how body, soul and spirit develop their own particular demands or avoidances in the process of supporting and tolerating each other. These were — and still are — very far-reaching experiences.[87]

The Camphill friends experienced Karl König as milder in temperament, more loving and more brotherly after the illness that he had such difficulty in overcoming. Liberated from many everyday responsibilities König decided to start extensive writing. He drafted a substantial pioneering monograph on Down's syndrome and a publication about the first three years of child development as well as numerous further studies. At the same time König continued to participate in the development of the Camphill movement. König also gave his full support to the new phase of the Camphill movement's development, encouraging the establishment of a village community in northern England, Botton, where adults with special needs would live and work together with so-called healthy adults, and, according to König, would thus realize together the development of a new social form for the future.

During the course of an immensely successful journey drawing large public audiences to South Africa in spring 1957, König was central in creating the conditions for yet further groups to become active within the Camphill movement and for curative education facilities to be established there. König emphasized in a letter that the attempt must be made to establish 'a piece of Europe' everywhere in the world, 'so that we can gradually realize the unfulfilled intention of the German nation throughout the world.'[88] This statement shows that König considered the task of the Camphill movement to be the active pursuit of the intentions that had gone adrift as a consequence of the collapse of Central Europe, especially those of Germany and of the Anthroposophical Society. In König's opinion Rudolf Steiner

had not intended an elitist philosophy group for the bourgeois middle class but a cosmopolitan, therapeutic initiative; in this way König had also experienced Ita Wegman's work after March 30, 1925. As ever he still felt an innermost commitment for her.

Karl König's second voyage to South Africa in February 1961 took place during a noteworthy date. While on the freighter he wrote the story of Camphill on the hundredth anniversary of Rudolf Steiner's birth. König's story — called 'The Candle on the Hill' — recalled his Advent experiences at Arlesheim and concluded with the following words in memory of Rudolf Steiner: 'My heart is filled with reverence and gratitude for this destiny which led me to work in the name of this great man.'[89] König also studied Steiner's autobiography while travelling on the small freighter in the Atlantic. He arrived in South Africa on March 4, the anniversay of Ita Wegman's death. In her spirit König wanted to work in Africa.

Karl König's second visit to South Africa was also immensely fruitful, both for his own endeavours and for the Camphill movement. König spoke to the South African parliament about the education of children with severe handicaps and he also actively participated in a medical symposium focusing on the treatment of psychosis in children and adolescents. His profound knowledge of these medical fields was highly esteemed, as was his representation of a new ethic that should be developed for the treatment of people suffering from innate disabilities and problems. König also engaged in the social and political issues of South Africa, with great concern but in view of the developments to come:

> Is it not so that in South Africa at present, where white people have to acknowledge their grave mistakes of the past, suffering — not tyranny — will prevail? Perhaps in this very place where European arrogance and nationalism will be presented with a statement of their debts, the 'creditors' will forgive them, cancel what is owing and say: If you are willing, friend, here is my hand. Let us live together in peace and brotherhood.[90]

In 1961 Frederik Willem Zeylmans van Emmichoven, a Dutch psychiatrist, also visited South Africa for the second time. Zeylmans was close to Ita Wegman who, together with König, had been present at the opening of his clinic in the Hague in summer 1928. Zeylmans had intentions which were related to those of König — a cosmopolitan social mission of anthroposophy in the age of Michael.

Zeylmans did not establish any Camphill communities but as an esoteric anthroposophist of international standing he took Rudolf Steiner's Foundation Stone Meditation to countless places all over the word. Zeylmans' lectures, too, were extraordinarily well attended and of immediate effect. But on his second

* Hermanus, the first Camphill community in South Africa.

Africa journey Willem Zeylmans van Emmichoven unexpectedly died in Cape Town. König, who was already back in Camphill by this time, was deeply moved by this event. Two weeks after Zeylmans' cremation he wrote to Eberhard Schickler:

> Seldom has the death of a friend stirred me as deeply as this sudden and unexpected passing. ... I dreamt of him continuously during the night from Saturday to Sunday. I was in Cape Town and he showed me the place where he died and then said (he spoke in English): 'People believe that I am dead, but I have never been so alive.' He also said many other things and revealed his real name to me — I must tell you about that sometime in person. Above all, I am thankful that he had just been at Hermanus* and spent two very harmonious days there with us. ... So something previously unresolved between us could be clarified. His departure is an irreplaceable loss for the Anthroposophical Society. It is as though one of the last true 'men of the world' amongst us has now gone. ... It is becoming lonely here and still one must continue until one's own call of destiny sounds.[91]

*

Zeylmans had visited the United States in 1948 and 1950 and through many encounters and lecturing experiences there, had formed his own idea of the potential of the American people and also of where the dangers lay for the nation. This he expressed in a publication from 1950 entitled *Amerika en het Amerikanismus* (America and Americanism). Karl König himself travelled twice more to the United States (in 1960 and 1962) where he gave a series of important lectures and made preparations for founding new Camphill communities. Like Zeylmans ten years earlier, König wrote about the significance of America and particularly about the positive aspects of the country's potential for

development. In an essay entitled *Amerika, hast du es besser?* (America, are things better for you?) he declared that he had never before encountered a nation with such capacity for fraternity as America. According to König, America was the place where the essence of Rudolf Steiner's Fundamental Social Law could come into its own — thus dissolving 'the terrible marriage between work and wages.' König also believed that a great number of Americans would be willing to fight for human dignity. Throughout his visits he had the impression that the United States was a nation 'on trial by God': God was testing 'the capacities of a nation that he expects will lead humankind into a better future.'[92] König incisively pointed out (as had Zeylmans) that the future of America would depend on the participation of Europe. It was necessary for Europe to understand that the 'decisive battles' of the twentieth and twenty-first centuries would take place in America.

> If spirituality is not strengthened over there so that many hundred, indeed thousands of young Europeans carry across the seeds of a *new,* practical rather than merely theoretical spiritual science, founding spiritual centres in future decades and becoming doctors, teachers, farmers, curative educationalists and artists serving the growing need there; if this does not come about in some form, it is hardly possible to predict what will happen.[93]

It was Ita Wegman, who, already in the 1920s and at the beginning of the 1930s, together with Daniel Nicol Dunlop, repeatedly drew anthroposophists' attention to the crucial shift towards the West. (According to Liane Collot d'Herbois in 1939 Wegman had considered moving to Canada to start a clinic in Vancouver.) The doctors Eugen Kolisko, Willem Zeylmans and Karl König belonged to that group of individuals who continually attempted to work towards this goal. König contributed to the endeavour by establishing the Camphill curative education communities in America.

★

At the beginning of the sixties, Karl König participated with renewed energy in events in Germany. He spoke to eight hundred people at the University of Berlin about curative education He lectured frequently on the thalidomide catastrophe and on euthanasia, as well as on the mission and the particular dignity of children with special needs.

Hans Müller-Wiedemann described the impression that Karl König made in Germany after 1945 — this émigré Jew and expelled anthroposophist who had meanwhile founded an effective curative education movement in Scotland.

> Who was this man — this emigrant — who, during wartime, had build up a community in the British Isles and now, in the aftermath of the war, began to speak publicly in Germany? Many found their answer to this question (posed frequently during the first years after the war) in rumours and assumptions. König was a kind of mythological character — a foreign, legendary figure with enormous powers of persuasion and eloquence. Only gradually could one begin to form a true impression of the nature of Camphill and who Karl König was. For there were many rumours, both enthusiastic approval and suspicious rejection. Not least, it was due to König's travels to Germany that a large number of young seekers, who, as children or teenagers, had experienced Nazism during wartime, joined the group around König in Scotland after the war — bringing about a remarkable, often dramatic and fruitful encounter between Jewish survivors, and those who had escaped with their lives from the Nazis and come through the war. This kind of encounter, so it appeared, could only take place in the light of anthroposophy. This aspect of Camphill life in those early post-war years,

> although veiled beneath the surface of daily life and not openly spoken about, gave the community the character of a continual healing of wounds of destiny.
>
> An extraordinary and deeply spiritual mood arose. ... Essential aspects of Central European culture had penetrated even the smallest details of everyday life at Camphill all those years, and were thereby saved from extermination and later served the new impulses of those who came as seekers. The spiritually-imbued hope cultivated in Camphill life during the war years was the source that König drew on when he attempted to work in the German-speaking world after the war. The Central Europe that had gone into exile now spoke through him and began to be noticed again. His intentions went far beyond the establishing of Camphill centres in Germany, and indeed this was not the primary aim of his endeavours. Even though König wore the mantle of Camphill wherever he went, his own personal karma — which had deep historical antecedents connecting him to Central Europe — became more and more transparent through his work in Germany after the war. For him, the path to the West was predestined and had to be taken, and outer events had supported this course. Yet König never felt at home in the West and the ancient spiritual heritage of Central Europe which lived in him (Prague at its heart) called him back again after the war to attend to particular tasks.[94]

In fact, Karl König finally moved to Brachenreuthe near Lake Constance in March 1964 and spent the remaining two years of his life in Germany.

From there König continued to work tirelessly. He lectured about the task of curative education in the twentieth century and the social predicament of humanity, and continued his spiritual studies. He travelled to Prague and visited Karlstein Castle. He deeply absorbed the underlying spiritual concept of this building. In October 1964 he gave a series of lectures entitle 'Eternal Youth' in Vienna, the city of his birth.

At the same time König continued regular medical therapeutic work. By this time he was an eminent and highly sought-after anthroposophical curative doctor. Countless children and parents came to him, not only seeking appropriate medical treatment but also wanting to understand more about the path of destiny of people facing incarnation difficulties within a society driven by economics and achievement. These meetings and consultations became increasingly difficult for König. In his journal he wrote: 'In the consultations, hardship after hardship follow misery upon misery. Sometimes their grief is so close to the surface, I can hardly hold back my distress and tears. ... The Janus head of the German economic miracle.'[95] At the end of November 1965 he said: 'I am becoming anxious about the sheer numbers of destinies presented to me daily, each demanding a response. ... How will my over-tired heart be able to cope with it all?'[96]

In 1965 König held succesful lectures on curative education diagnostics in Berlin, and he also produced numerous important written works, including one about the anthroposophical *Soul Calendar,* studies of the animal world, crucial biographical turning points of the nineteenth century and the story of the Camphill movement. He recorded the following about his curative education lectures in Berlin: 'Many new insights arise and everything comes to me immediately, as mature fruit. Is this not like a song of farewell? Will I no longer manage to write a textbook about all of this? I sense a great weariness in my heart.'[97]

Although König increasingly suffered from serious heart problems, he still managed to visit the island of Reichenau at Lake Constance at the end of 1965 where he researched the history of an Irish monastery. This was a most moving experience for him considering that the Camphill communities had been founded in the same area — at Brachenreuthe and Föhrenbühl.

Destiny had led König to bring the curative educational movement to the North West, to the landscape of the Hibernian Mysteries and the realms of Celtic Christianity; now it was also at home in Central Europe, in the Lake Constance area which had received and assimilated Irish Christian culture a thousand years before.

Towards the end of his life, König occupied himself with the history and destiny of the Jewish people, a crucial factor in his own biography which had influenced his destiny in the twentieth century. Throughout his life König had considered the conditions and preconditions of the event of Christ which was the focus of his interest and work. The question of the Jewish religion, its task and its destiny had always been on his mind, but at the end of his life this question regained momentum. König himself cited an event on December 11, 1963 that precipitated his intensified study of the mission and destiny of the Jewish people. While speaking at a Bible Evening he discovered that the text of the Mount of Olives apocalypse, the 'Little Apocalypse' in St Matthew's Gospel, is not a prediction for humanity as a whole but a prophecy of the future destiny of the Jewish people. König held further lectures on this theme at Lake Constance at the end of 1965 and in January 1966 at Camphill.

Karl König spent New Year of 1965/66 in Scotland where he spoke about the 'Constellation of the Stars in the Cosmic Heart.' In March he was in Germany lecturing once more about euthanasia, aspects of destiny and biography, and about the 'Gate of the Moon and the Gate of the Sun.' König held another outstanding course on embryology in Freiburg on March 12 and 13, 1966. A week later he was in Dornach to prepare for a medical conference that would take place in the coming year where he wanted to speak about the problems of epilepsy and psychosis. König, excluded from Dornach since 1935, had held numerous meetings and conversations with the Executive Council of the General Anthropsophical Society over many years with the purpose of establishing links to the Camphill movement, which had been founded during the years of exile. In 1965 König wrote in one of this letters: 'I am deeply committed to bringing about an integration of the Camphill community with the General Anthroposophical Society.'[98]

On March 21, 1966, six days before his death, Karl König wrote to Margit Engel: 'Many journeys still lie ahead — most important of all, a trip to East Germany where Leipzig University has formally invited me to give lectures about Camphill. From there I will travel to Dresden, Prague, Budapest and Vienna so that the endeavour in the East can truly begin.'[99] With invitations to East Germany, Czechoslovakia and Hungary the way to the East opened, to the spiritual landscape which he had recognized as his ancient home; where he had begun his work and where he had seen great tasks for the future. König was unable to take this path, however. Only days after this last letter he suffered a massive heart attack and was taken to Überlingen Hospital at Lake Constance. It was Karl König's heart that failed — the organ of destiny and conscience he had studied in such great depth; the organ that had carried him through his unceasing work every day until total exhaustion. 'I am becoming anxious about the sheer numbers of destinies presented to me daily, each demanding a response. ... How will my over-tired heart be able to cope with it all?'[100]

Around midday on Sunday, March 27, 1966 Karl König passed through the Gate of Death and the 'Gate of the Sun.' The first part of the funeral was at Ita Wegman House in Föhrenbühl, a Camphill community near Lake Constance, led by Georg and Erika von Arnim and on which he had put great hopes — as he had on the curative education movement in general.

> We must have a sufficiently broad understanding of the idea of curative education if we are to perceive its true significance. It seeks to become a worldwide activity, so that in a truly helpful way it may counteract threats to the individual that are now apparent everywhere. The 'curative education attitude' must come to expression in all social work, in pastoral care, in the care of the elderly, in the rehabilitation of the mentally ill and of the physically handicapped, in the care of orphans and refugees, and of those in despair or contemplating suicide.[101]

Anke Weihs

Life with Dr König

Anke Weihs

For those who have lived and worked with Dr König in the Camphill movement since its beginnings, it is not easy to state, to document the tribute one would like to pay, or to impart something of the peculiar quality of his existence as a leader, teacher and friend.

Yet to the stream of tributes that are appearing in a number of journals and papers in English and in German, belong no doubt the little tributaries that flow from the more intimate places of day-to-day existence to enrich the broader stream of the survey of his life's work.

I shall not hesitate to be personal.

I met Dr König in 1938 in Vienna where as a young person I suffered from a persistent form of allergy which leading specialists and professors had been unable to help. An acquaintance, a medical student who was a member of Dr König's Youth Group, advised me to go to Dr König. Other friends were deeply perturbed at this idea — for was not the method practised synonymous with spiritism and the like? with dark rooms and abracadabra? They tried their best to prevent me from going to 'that man.'

Nonetheless, despair drove me to the telephone to make an appointment with 'that man.' It was not easy to get one; his time was booked up far in advance. The assistant finally told me to come at three o'clock in the afternoon ten days hence.

Dr König had a house in a beautiful residential part of Vienna some distance from the centre. A venerable tram took you along beneath the boughs of chestnut trees past banks of lilac bushes and the flowering shrubs so characteristic of that city. The house stood on a corner. It seemed quiet; the entrance hall was light the waiting room in no way suggestive of anything but a certain peace. Cane covered benches stood around the walls and between them were aquaria containing a great variety of small unusual fish. It was evident that the owner of the house was a lover of the creature.

The waiting-room was packed to capacity with waiting patients. As the afternoon wore on — my own hour had long struck — the room grew more and more crowded. A seemingly unending stream of patients came, disappeared within to leave by another door. Some were given priority, others waited. The hours passed. The periodic click of the automatic water refreshener in the aquaria marked the march of time. I resolved a few times to get up and go — if all these people in the room were to be seen before me?

Towards evening my name was called. I rose stiffly and passed the many still sitting on the benches, and entered a tiny room where an assistant took details, then a door to a further room was opened — I went through and was inside.

The last glow of the setting sun came in through the windows and filled the room. At the desk in the centre stood a very small man with a large — a lion's — head. He wore a physician's white coat. His eyes were very big and grave. When they rested on you, they did not only see through you, they seemed to create you anew. Something dormant in yourself responded whether you wanted it to or not; you seemed to become what you really were, beneath the layers of habit, inhibition and illusion.

This peculiar gaze, I think, was one of the unique characteristics in Dr König. I would call it a 'creative gaze.' He not only saw what you were but what you were meant to be.

There are people who can study you, see through you, recognize the forces at work, but there are few who can 'create' you. We may struggle to remind ourselves when we regard another person that a spark of the divine lives in him as well — indeed this is a facet of the discipline that arises from the pursuit of anthroposophy. But although this discipline no doubt clears the way to the other person, it is not necessarily an outpouring of warmth, a living flow from one person to another.

In Dr König the gaze was a channel for the flow of warmth, it was in itself healing, for one felt one was seen in one's hidden truth, and always with respect and compassion.

I think this first grave gaze — Dr König otherwise said little — was the initial step in healing. The medicines that followed were effective because something in the inner situation had begun to change — whereby I felt no onrush of sympathy or *Schwärmerei* for this small doctor — I only felt called up, impersonally, to my better self.

This was the experience of those who encountered Dr König as a physician, and as indicated, his practice in Vienna was large, as it had been before in Silesia.

To this same gaze, our handicapped children responded powerfully. Dr König was not a bit sentimental and he expected the most, even of a disabled child. He could be forbidding when a child 'played up.' But the moment the grave look with its beam of warmth touched the core of the most disturbed child, it responded like a flower. opening up and showing the beauty within.

The peculiar power to call people up to their better selves and thus to create the first condition for healing reminded one of Socrates' description of himself as a 'midwife,' helping to bring to birth the higher self in the other.

This small doctor in the physician's white coat was a practicer of 'spiritual midwifery' throughout his life, and many 'spiritual children' owe their emergence to him.

Needless to say, the medicines prescribed did their work and the chronic ailment suffered since childhood disappeared within three weeks.

A few years later when Camphill had already started, we had an outbreak of the disentery that went through the country during the early stages of the war. I had a group of four small boys, all of whom were severely ill with temperatures of 106°F (41°C). There were anxious sleepless nights and the little boys lay listless and emaciated in their beds. Dr König had been away. Our official medical officer from the nearby village had been attending. On the morning of his return, Dr König came over to see the patients; there were many more. Upon entering the house, he sniffed. We too had noticed the strange sweet smell of disease. 'Hang up sheets dipped in lavender or rosemary — the illness thrives on its smell,' was all he said. We found nothing but eucalyptus and soon drenched sheets were hanging up all over the house.

By the early afternoon the illness had taken a turn, temperatures went down, symptoms receded, and the next day recovery was under way.

There is an account of how Hippocrates turned the tide of the plague in Athens through similar means. Not that I want to say that Dr König was atavistic or unscientific. He was neither. Few men were so well informed as to the medical developments of his own time and he never hesitated to acclaim or make use of what he found valuable in modern scientific research. He was only a physician by virtue of all his powers — his knowledge, his empathy, his therapeutic fire, his intuition, his intense self-discipline, his morality. He was Hippocratic in a truly modern sense. He adjusted the basic situation for the wholeness of the person to re-establish.

We had among our pupils at Murtle an eleven-year-old boy with a severe convulsive condition, very retarded and who suffered as well from a massive eczema which encrusted his whole body. His skin was like scales. This latter condition seemed to be brought on by fish — not even eating fish but by the mere presence of fish in the house. Therefore on days when the rest of the household ate fish, Ian had to be kept upstairs in the nursery. Even so his skin would get red and tight all over and cause him much distress.

One day when Dr König examined Ian and we all had expressed our concern about his condition, Dr König said he knew Ian's treatment — he was to have a spoonful of the juice extracted from the muscles of salmon three times a week. We were all horrified. Who would dare once again to impress it upon Dr König that the mere presence of fish in the house ...? 'See that you get this juice and begin treatment straightaway.'

So Scotland was turned upside down — it was not the season for salmon — to procure enough of the right parts from which to extract the prescribed juice. Ian's father was very helpful. Feeling that we were going to be murderers, we gave Ian his first spoonful of 'salmon juice.' Nothing happened, not even the slightest redness and in a few weeks Ian was not only able to tolerate the presence of fish but to eat it, and for the first time in his life to be free of eczema and develop a soft pliable skin all over his body. His convulsive disorder was also relieved to a certain extent.

These were flashes of a genius that was no doubt very much Dr König's own. He only had the courage to consider such flashes, also in others, as real as the medicine bottle and to act accordingly. Thus he was able to give indescribable and lasting relief to so many of his patients.

When Dr König found himself in a bleak Scottish manse in the early spring of 1939, exiled from his own country, with a small group of young people with whom he was to build up a place for handicapped children and an own way of community living, one wonders what he felt.

Although he was small in stature, one always had the sense of greatness, of lionhood; his ideals and impulses had lion dimensions There was nothing of the tender hesitant dreamer. His were full-blooded and convinced impulses to fight and to conquer. And now these reduced circumstances, this obscurity, this strange language, this being an 'enemy alien,' these egoistic, unknowledgeable young people, so utterly untrained, as the only collaborators of himself and his wife! Here Dr König was a master. For he always accepted the given circumstances, however modest, but in accepting them did not 'suffer' them. He created a new set of circumstances on a human and spiritual level which either made the external set of circumstances no longer necessary or transformed them from within.

Dr König had a unique power of accepting people.

Generally exacting in his relation to people, he had the remarkable gift to let them be and to accept any new 'odd' young person with a kind of expectancy peculiar to himself.

Early on in Vienna, two young arrogant and 'free thinking' medical students from the University came to the lectures he gave in his own house. They did not make a reassuring impression on the other members of the Youth Group Dr König had established. Their attitude to so many things the Youth Group held high seemed questionable. Yet these two and the friends who followed them were recognized and accepted by Dr König himself.

This was the group that went with him into exile.

As this group grew in responsibilities in the coming years, Dr König placed each one in leading positions in the expanding Movement. Yet he never relied solely on his 'old generals;' he always looked into the future, saw the wish to serve in the young and drew it forth. He created a kind of 'spiritual-social democracy' which ideally makes use of the specific powers of all age-groups and builds on the willingness to serve rather than on the laurels already achieved. Thus a 'senate' of the greyer heads was never a characteristic of Camphill.

As a teacher Dr König was strict, exacting, often intolerant. The lion's voice could often be heard through the house when an unfortunate had left a dustpan lying somewhere, it possibly being the first time in that particular unfortunate's life that he had even handled a dustpan!

The same intolerance was shown when relationships became untidy, motives confused. Dr König had an outstanding power to create and maintain order. He was not pedantic, he was only orderly and abhorred disorder. Basic order was the foundation for a cultural way of life. Community living must be cultural living. Where standards and tastes lack form and discrimination, these must be taught. So everything we did, from the library to the back door, came under scrutiny. Wild horses felt the bridle for the first time. It was not always easy.

Yet never once in any situation whatsoever in all the long years of living with Dr König did we ever witness a lax moment, a disorderly corner around his own person, a hurriedly abandoned writing desk, stacks of loose papers or books left lying at random. Everything was in absolute order up to the last moment of his life as though at any time he might be called away.

Of his thousands of books, he knew the exact place of each. Sometimes when we had a meeting with him downstairs in Camphill House in what is called the Camphill Goethe Library, one might notice him suddenly, in the midst of a conversation, staring into the distance, not listening. When you followed up his intent gaze, you saw it did not rest on a distant horizon at all! It rested on a misplaced book somewhere up on the highest shelf! And the inevitable storm burst!

The same powerful sense of order was not only related to the things with which he lived; it was equally related to his use of time. He was extremely punctual and would not accept unpunctuality in others. There was no gentle schooling in punctuality for those more handicapped in this subject! Either you came on time or you put yourself outside. Doors to lectures, meetings and the like were shut on the dot of the determined hour and woe betide the later comer. Happily, or as a result, latecomers are rather rare in Camphill.

Punctuality is not only a 'good habit,' a considerate attitude; it is the magic key that opens up the mystery of time. An hour can be an infinite well of enlightenment if it starts 'on time.' The same hour can be utterly unfruitful if the edges are frayed by late coming. Punctuality is not only a form, it is a condition for activity.

Punctuality shows another thing. It is indicative that the individual is prepared for what is coming. He has adjusted his mind and his time in order to participate in the next thing. When he comes late, his mind is obviously not adjusted but in a state of disorder, and he will need a good part of the meeting or lecture to establish equilibrium and to make either an active or passive contribution.

Dr König was an example of careful preparation. Leaving the fulfilment of a meeting, a talk, entirely open to the coming event, he was nonetheless prepared. He laid aside other issues, cleared his mind and was simply ready to receive. He never came to a meeting looking as though he were preoccupied with something else or burdened by something 'more important.' Nothing was ever more important than the issue at hand, whatever its nature.

Lectures were carefully prepared, although speaking came easily to him, but a lecture is a responsible act like any other. And in bringing about big moves or ventures in the Camphill movement, he never did things hurriedly, however urgent. He let things develop, ripen. He had the ability to wait, to turn over the soil, to let other factors take their course. He had 'sweeping' ideas, but his implementation was always circumspect, responsible and selfless.

Dr König wore a gold pocket watch with a chain that wound through the buttonholes of his waistcoat. The watch would be drawn out of its resting place, there would be the slightly sideways turn of the head to look at it and it would be returned to the pocket. This was always a gentle unassuming gesture, but no less telling. The time had come!

Dr König was a busy man but never in haste. His output on all levels far exceeded the ordinary. Yet relaxation belonged to activity and he always found time for it. At his table, conversation was usually lively. But he could sometimes be bored — a lion's yawn might be the only reaction to something you thought very significant. He was at times an *enfant terrible,* but he had as well a delightful and redeeming sense of humour. For he was an Austrian, a Viennese, and possessed all the charm and whimsy, the *Mutterwitz,* of that particular group. He would sometimes lapse into the vernacular and pour forth delightfully outrageous remarks on anything and anyone. He demanded great earnestness where earnestness was appropriate, but he could ridicule the 'long face' in no uncertain terms. Laughter is as essential to community living as anything else.

Fitted into his time, there was the prodigious reading, both literary and scientific, his own writing, his unceasing research, his animal studies, the enormous correspondence, the many meetings, college meetings and the like necessitated by our therapeutic work, and his talks.

These were talks with us, later with parents, with people who came for advice in all kinds of situations, sometimes from far distances, and then again with the increasing numbers of people who came to work at Camphill, including the very young.

These were talks a person had about himself, his problems, with a listening man. But they were not only confessional. Dr König was never content with a mere unburdening. The talk was always decisive. When it was over you were not only unburdened, you had with his help made resolves.

Again this is rather unique. There are people one likes to talk to, to 'confess' to, and their interest and sympathy are always agreeable. But so often you come away still not knowing what to do, which way to go. Dr König did not always show either interest or sympathy. An intensely musical person, he reacted accordingly when you started off on a wrong or false note, when he sensed affectation, arbitrary attitudes. All too soon would the lion's roar be provoked. But after the thunderstorm if you were willing, there would be gentleness, helpfulness, a steady rising of hope and a new beginning.

In the early years of Camphill, Dr König was superintendent as well as doctor for the school which was rapidly expanding. Sitting at his desk, dictating innumerable letters, he was there for everything, for every call, any question as to how to go on. For we had no one else to ask — how to teach, to look after a child, to deal with a convulsion, to paint, to garden, to treat a sick horse, when to do this and to do that.

He administered the finances with care and circumspection yet keenly — often there was little to administer — but it was always in hand. He knew every corner of the estate, every nook in the house. There were frequent visitors, constant comings of parents of children.

Yet all this seemed to be a relatively minor part of his existence.

Already in the old manse in the north he had begun our 'education.' This happened on different levels. I remember the long winter evenings when we gathered in his study downstairs around the tiny open fireplace. The curtains heaving with draughts behind us, and we had to stand up and recite poems, long ones and short ones, and accompany our efforts with gestures! But there was no escape. Yet Dr König himself was a natural example of co-ordinated movement. For although he was unusually small, his feet having a slight impairment since birth, his bearing was remarkably free and there was a hidden grace in his gait.

When Dr König lectured, he paced to and for, the words seemed to come with his strides. When he spoke about animals, a dear subject, he would with one characteristic gesture become one or the other animal, to the infinite delight of his audience.

With us, he studied historical periods, personalities, the lives of men who had inaugurated impulses, curative or social. We were given tasks of our own to study and early on were encouraged to 'lecture' to the others.

We were taught to have interests and to share them I remember well how angry Dr König could be if any of us had read an interesting book and had not told the others about it, and equally how infuriated he was if we had not read a valuable new publication but had let it slip past.

He himself shared all his interests, which were very manifold and constantly new, stimulating us never to become stagnant. There is a problem in many people's minds about community living: you have to give up your private interests and serve only those of the group. Inevitably this is a stage one goes through in community living. Yet Dr König himself never had this problem. His was a rich personal life conducted with a full sense of personal freedom, but he was both responsible as well as generous. He shared his spiritual pleasures to the last drop and enriched others at the same time. He was never the poorer through having given so much.

It can well be said that the many conferences in the Camphill movement are the results of this trait in Dr König. Their themes were all personal interests of his who made them the basis for wider study. It was his love of spiritual, social pioneering, of adventure in the field of therapy that formed the foundation of the many symposia that have furthered our work.

Man is, however private, a social being, Dr König would quote time and again. If he is not fully both, he is only part of what he is meant to be. Therefore, Dr König deplored talk of 'private life' as an objection to community living.

None of the young people who formed Dr König's little army in 1939 had much notion of Rudolf Steiner's teaching, for some it was alien. Yet he himself based all his work and striving on Rudolf Steiner's teaching and knew that his future work for handicapped children would at all times have to flow from that source and no other. Therefore his young helpers would have to become pupils of Rudolf Steiner. But there was no force or coercion — simply a knowledge that as our destinies had led us to him, we would have to wake up to the fact that working with him meant — with Rudolf Steiner.

So Dr König steadfastly studied basic books and lectures with us, leading us step by step into a new world. In this world, he himself moved freely, was always creative, forward-going, courageous, and at the same time, he had an infallible way of preserving the integrity of Rudolf Steiner's spiritual science. His own strong devotion to his teacher was teaching for us. He kindled that devotion in us as well, not to himself, but to Rudolf Steiner.

But the accumulation of spiritual information and facts was not enough for Dr König, although he himself knew every single lecture that Rudolf Steiner had given, and there are thousands. It is better to make one thing one's own than to swallow everything at a gulp. He taught us never to live by theory, but to regard every minute of the day as an exercise in devotion, humility, creativity and the willingness to change oneself. 'Change your ways' — the clarion call of John the Baptist was the challenge to which we were perhaps most affined in the years Camphill was being built up.

As a personal teacher or mentor of Rudolf Steiner's spiritual science, Dr König was patient, understanding, encouraging where there was an earnest effort. He could be wellnigh devastating when he felt you were playing about or given to misuse. His wrath had the same peculiar quality as his other characteristics; it gave you back your own. It established your equilibrium. It was never a mere giving vent to his own displeasure. I think a measure of 'divine wrath' was given to him to use in this life for the moulding of others.

You could never go to Dr König to complain about others. You got nowhere when you did. Instead of bringing shame on the other, you brought it on yourself. The change in his facial expression when you tried to complain about someone was enough to announce a disaster if you persisted. He disliked a 'worm's view' of the other person and regarded the summing up of another person's 'complexes' as nothing but an excuse for one's own falling short of human obligations. His reaction to a breakdown in human relationships amongst us was stern. Nor would he ever mediate; he demanded the direct encounter to put things straight.

He himself never fell short of at least taking on the whole burden another person presented. This carrying of other people's burdens was at times heroic and many have experienced his extraordinary sustaining strength.

It was not that Dr König never failed. He failed often and had the courage to fail, for he would always take risks, was never cautious, rather trustful in his dealings with other people. His failures lay more frequently than not in his high expectation of the other, his demand on their best powers — something some people might call 'overestimation.' He was generous in his hopes, but when disappointed he often found it difficult to forgive, to establish a new relationship. He was fairly absolute.

There are many people outside Camphill and some who at times were here who felt that Dr König was imperious, that he did not respect personal freedom but expected everyone to submit to him and his aims and that those who worked with him were blind followers.

Dr König no doubt did not make it easy for the individual to establish his own freedom. He could not brook selfishness and illusion. You had to go through the eye of the needle and the freedom you achieved had to be real freedom which does not mean opposition. When he saw even the smallest glimmer of true freedom in the other, he was the first to acclaim it, to foster it and to build on it to the infinite benefit of all.

He was no doubt imperious, imperious as the lion, and things mostly had to go his way. His way was usually a considered one, more often both wise and good. But two things especially made it possible for others to live with this trait: He was entirely able to accept, if not opposition, then fair correction and would readily consider the other person's view and make it his own. For so powerful and self-contained a person he was surprisingly open to correction.

Finally, all those who lived and worked with him for so long a time were witnesses of the unrelenting struggle he had with himself to make this lion a lamb. His brave battle with everything that was imperious in himself, with his confessed love of the red carpet that sought for the central and perhaps omnipotent place, in order to develop humility, was to those who beheld it, truly heroic. It was a struggle of years and in the last few of his life, many circles inside and outside Camphill felt the fruits of this struggle, experienced the balsam of his humility, were sustained by the example of a 'great servant.'

Therefore, when Rudolf Meyer, the priest of the Christian Community who celebrated the funeral service for Dr König at the Lake of Constance, spoke of him as having been a brother to his fellow men, he set a seal on the long brave way Dr König had gone in the singular overcoming of himself.

A remarkable gift of Dr König's was his ability to delegate. Imperious on the one hand and preferring to do things himself, in the deeper more vital spheres of the life of the Camphill movement, he knew how to delegate and to foster responsibility and carrying power in others. Thus when Dr König died, the widespread Camphill movement was so organized and ordered and functions were so carefully delegated that no thought had to cross our minds that the work he had begun could not carry on. The hole he left in our midst has been full of hope and strength instead of being an aching gap, which it could have been.

To be able to delegate must finally be the ability to face death with creativity and courage, even with love, because one knows that whatever one lets go freely and with trust, will return in fuller measure and that only if one lets go, does not hoard, will new life be engendered.

Dr König was one of those people who are becoming rarer in our time — a universal person. He not only had a variety of interests but also a variety of gifts. He drew, wrote poems and plays, too. The poems are perhaps the least known, except for those published in a little book by some friends at the occasion of his sixtieth birthday. They contain profound thoughts, and a beauty and depth which are surprising even for those who knew him well. He played the piano in earlier years but never very well. Yet — and this is perhaps a predominant feature in his personality — he was outstandingly musical. His sense of music was manifest in everything he did. When you sat at a meeting — it could have been an ordinary meeting about daily affairs or any other meeting — and he was in the chair, you often felt that this was a chamber orchestra and he the conductor. At first the theme sounded, then the variations came, the andantes, allegros, and finally the ultimate musical statement. This power of his to invest human dealings with musical experience made meetings alive, fruitful, and even when they had to deal with problems, they always reached the finale. His 'conducting' allowed a whole range of human ideas, sentiments, intentions, and all the different instruments to express themselves. There was never anything perfunctory, nominal, in any meeting chaired by Dr König. His intuitive knowing how far to go, when to stop a discussion was basically musical. I often had occasion to think of his lectures as sonatas, so musically were they built up.

Although his own personal musical tastes were varied, they had a strong leaning to Mahler. But it was inevitably Beethoven of whom one thought when one lived in Dr König's vicinity. The full-bloodedness, the width, height and breadth of feeling, the lyrical moments, the roundness and basic sense of harmony as well as the suggestion of titanic dimensions were all his.

The likeness to Beethoven was very much in our minds when

we saw Dr König on the evening of the day he died. Similar to the circumstances accompanying Beethoven's death on March 26 in 1827, so also was Dr König's death on March 27, 1966 accompanied by the unleashing of the elements. A wild storm raged.

Dr König once said that the slow movement of the Fourth Piano Concerto of Beethoven described in music the supremacy of the ego of man over all the threats, the floods of darkness that surround him. This supremacy, however, is based on gentleness and humility and infinite human tenderness.

While the wild storm raged that night, not only over the Lake of Constance but over the whole of Europe, Dr König lay still, his features younger and determined, and as though he would say: it is all right — I have managed this too. A certain element of light was around him.

This slow movement of Beethoven's, where the flower-like single One faces the oncoming betrayers in a kind of Gethsemane ends with a musical statement that sounds like the words of Christ in John (16:33): 'Be of good cheer, I have overcome the world.'

This brings me to the essential in Dr König — he was a servant of Christ. When the Name of Christ first pricked him, it did not merely scratch the surface, it went deep into his existence. In this sense, he was Pauline — he 'put on the whole armour of God.'

His intuitive powers enabled him to know more, to see more than most other men. What he knew and saw was the meaning of Christ for mankind as it was taught at the beginning of the century by Rudolf Steiner. His life was the life of a man who has been called — called for the benefit of his fellows.

Hans-Heinrich Engel

Some Personal Memories

Hans-Heinrich Engel

To have met Dr König in one's lifetime was more than just coincidence; even more than destiny; it was grace. It was as if one was permitted to look with different eyes into the world, as if the realm of truth was laid open before one for short moments.

When I worked for a short time as a physician in the psychiatric hospital, Wiesneck in southern Germany, for the first time I heard the name, Dr König. He was far away in Scotland, and though it then seemed very unlikely that I should ever go to Scotland or have anything to do with curative education, his name remained ringing in my heart and indeed within a very short time it was to become a principal factor in my life and destiny.

When I finally met him at the occasion of a doctors' conference at Schwäbisch Gmünd in 1950 I was deeply impressed by his presence of mind, his straightforward courage, his extreme warmth and his understanding of his fellow man. At this very first meeting he confronted me with a few remarks about myself which I suppose would have deeply offended me if anyone else had dared to make them, but his deep, loving understanding of my situation and youthful illusions made these remarks become a healing medicine rather than an offence.

Half a year later I visited Camphill and decided to become a co-worker. I surely had little reason to do so outwardly. But as I listened to Dr König speaking in the seminar about subjects I thought I had completely mastered, I had to realize that here I had found my teacher, the master for whom I had been looking and searching through all my university years. Here was someone whose words sounded alive, whose thoughts were not shadows, but full of life and truth, whose daily life was filled with the practice of what he demanded of others. Here was truth.

So I became once again an apprentice. Throughout the next years I was permitted to meet Dr König almost daily. The main contacts to begin with were in the clinics, in the college meetings, the doctors' group, the lectures and often even at lunch. When I arrived at Camphill I believed that I had some life experience and medical experience. I soon learnt that this was merely the platform on which to build what was expected of me. In this process Dr König was the inspirer, the corrector and never satisfied as long as one seemed to be satisfied oneself. The aims were high, and training in courage and true love never ceased. One thing was sure, while he would never hesitate to confront one with the result of one's deed or failure, he did it in such a manner that one always had a new starting point.

His deep and selfless understanding of one's own often miserable situation opened one's eyes. New vistas appeared and new paths to be followed. This experience was enhanced every morning during the three hours of clinics when children were seen by all the doctors in the presence of teachers and nursery parents. His incredible ability to listen actively created within him a picture of the child and a few questions soon made the rest of us see the direction of his vision. As he greeted the child or dealt with it, a powerful experience of a true 'healer will' radiated from him, which reached not only the child but all the others around him as well. These daily experiences of Dr

König meeting the children were invaluable treasures in every respect, because again we could experience: Here the truth is revealing itself in the gesture, in the word, in the thought of this man. Here faith is creating self-understanding and certainty. His loving interest revealed that he was truly with you, while his insight and outlook contained justified hope. It was therefore no surprise to see the children react in the way they did.

In January 1955 Dr König became quite ill. Shortly before this one of those wondrous testing times of community life had necessitated a talk, which had helped me over a crucial point. But now the situation was reversed. He had asked me to come so he could hand over his seminar lessons to me, a task I did not feel prepared for and which, so I realized later, was one of those healing remedies of love that he applied to others. But I could not do this without realizing his great pain and suffering. Together with Alix Roth I was with him day and night during the next four months. Although he bore the discomfort, pain and anxiety in a truly human way, in our daily talks about further treatment I could divine his modesty and his tremendous insight into his illness as well as into world affairs and everything else around him. I could also sense his spiritual vision about which, however, he would rarely speak. Yet when one knew him well enough, it was not necessary to use many words, for contact of heart, this most precious gift to the ego of man, radiated strongly from him, even though he was weak and ill. One night after an unusually heavy attack, while witnessing his particular medical situation, he quoted, still in tears from pain, from Goethe's *Fairy Tale.*

> Love does not rule, love transforms,
> The more one wants to hold in one's hand, the more
> it slips away and in the end the hand is clenched
> in a spasm around a void.

Thursday March 24

Schlafe länger als sonst & wache auch gestärkt auf. Lese am Morgen mit grosser Anteilnahme den Vortrag, in dem R. Steiner das Weltengewitter des 15. Jhdts. beschreibt, in welchem die kosmische Intelligenz in die menschlichen Gehirne eingeprägt wird.

Empfinde das menschliche Herz als eine Art Opfer & möchte etwas darüber aufschreiben, aber mir fehlt der Mut. Es ist draussen trüb & neblig & ich lese den Tag über eine grössere Reihe medizinischer Zeitschriften durch & finde wenig Wesentliches. Aber die Zerrissenheit, Spezialisierung & Entmenschlichung, macht mich verzweifelt.

Dann fasse ich Mut & lese einen Artikel über Angina pectoris. Das hatte ich bisher nicht gewagt zu tun; das Herz klopft & der untere Mensch ist tief erregt, aber ich will es durchhalten & kann es dann auch. Das ist ein wichtiger Augenblick von Selbsterkenntnis der Krankheit. Muss dann viel darüber denken & komme meinen eigenen Abirrungen wieder ein Stück näher.

Later, after his gradual recovery, he began travelling again and for some time I was able to accompany him on some of his journeys on the Continent. There were talks, meetings, lectures, conferences and this frail being who had only just recovered began to find new ground and new ways. I remember one of his first lectures after he began again to speak: it was painful and somewhat disappointing. Where was this mighty power of the word? Where was the strength of conviction, the fire of enthusiasm, the immediacy of truth that could open hearts? But in the course of the next years something entirely new gradually grew and unfolded. All that we had known before was there again: knowledge, conviction, fire, truth, vision, creative thinking, but now a metamorphosis had taken place. Something had been intensified; his mildness and love pervaded his spirit-vision and knowledge more strongly and he reached the hearts in quite a different way than before. It appeared also that the connection to his teacher Rudolf Steiner had become still more intimate during

Opposite: Karl König's diary entry for March 24, 1955

I sleep longer than usual and I feel strengthened on waking up. During the morning I read with great interest the lecture where Rudolf Steiner describes the world thunderstorm in the when the cosmic intelligence is imprinted in the human brains.

I experience the human heart as a kind of sacrifice (offering) and would like to write about this, but I lack the courage. Outside it is grey and foggy and I read in the course of the day in several issues of medical journals, but find little that is of substance. The scatteredness, specialisation and de-humanisations cause much despair in me.

I then pick up courage and read an article about angina pectoris. Up to now I had not dared to do this; the heart beats and the lower part of the human constitution is stirred up profoundly. But I have the will to endure this and am able to do so eventually. This is an important moment of self-knowledge about the illness. I have to ponder about this a lot and come closer to my own aberrations.

those last years. At the same time also his relationship to us, his co-workers, was changing. Until then he had undoubtedly been our teacher, and for many, a father-being. But now he was becoming a friend, even a brother, and this increased with the years.

On one of our journeys we discovered that Gustav Mahler's Second Symphony, *The Resurrection,* was to be performed in Stuttgart. Fortunately we could still get tickets and that evening will never fade from my memory. The experience of this great work in the presence of Dr König, and later our talk, opened up the wealth of a new world, leading me ever farther. To visit Dijon with Dr König and find traces of the Order of the Golden Fleece, or to stand with him at Kaspar Hauser's grave and walk through Ansbach in his memory, or only a year ago to be introduced by Dr König into his native Vienna, especially into the Imperial Treasury, were utterly indescribable experiences. As one looked over Vienna from the Leopoldsberg and gazed into the distant Hungarian plain, the whole past of Vienna and the key role of the Austro-Hungarian Monarchy in Europe arose. One looked with different eyes, one listened with different ears and thereby not only learnt a great deal but also became a better person.

In the many personal connections which Dr König never shunned to take upon himself one important feature was his great conscience and responsibility in regard to dependence and independence. It could happen only too easily that a person would feel happy and secure in being guided by him. This he would tolerate for a certain time, but would use that time to put this person on to an inner path of self-recognition and inner discipline which would lead to increased objectivity and spiritual independence. Nothing was worse than claiming dependence on his judgment. There he could be most outspoken and would put anybody straight at any time.

He and Camphill never remained the same. Everything grew and changed all the time, often to a bewildering degree, especially for the newcomer or onlooker. But organic growth and an immediate understanding of changing conditions for the spiritual needs of the community of the Camphill movement kept him and us constantly alert, aware, ready and willing to transform ourselves. Thus Dr König remained always young and in reality grew stronger and stronger the more he changed and transformed himself. So it was no surprise to us when he handed over the responsibility of Camphill in 1957 to Dr Thomas Weihs, remaining chairman of the Camphill movement, or in 1964 when he even handed this over to the regional chairman, concentrating his own efforts on Central Europe as his last and special task.

At the end of August 1965 Dr König came for the last time to Glencraig and spent four days there which were the happiest I can remember. His wisdom and love radiated forth and one could feel deeply ashamed on the one hand but even more uplifted on the other. Our discussion of future plans and of handing over further responsibilities was embedded in his profound loving understanding of man's needs and his determination to serve the Good here on earth.

My last visit to Dr König four weeks before he passed over the threshold was quite an incredible experience. Throughout the last half-year a deeply moving transformation had taken place, and when I met him now once more, my heart almost trembled. Sitting opposite this man, this being who had meant so much to me, I felt that I had to be very tender and careful not to bring any ordinary problem to him. It was as if his goodness, his love of mankind, had expanded and formed a large heart around him through which one was permitted to meet directly the world of the Angels. In this last talk we spoke of the future of the Camphill movement and its Community, of our concern for the end of this century. Yet it was he who reminded me that we had to stop, since I had to drive off in order to catch my plane for Holland. It was not easy to leave as he stood there in the door of the Birkenhäusle. A beautiful sun had transformed the greyness of Ash Wednesday, as I walked down the hill he waved and looked at me with his smile-a smile so familiar and dear, so humble, yet now even greater and stronger in his transparent love.

On March 27, 1966, I was again at the Lake of Constance. This time it was a different meeting. Now it was as if his being confirmed to us what he had taught us all his life. Throughout those days we could feel as an immediate experience the Majesty of the Spirit-being of Man in the Love of Christ.

Appendix

Detailed Plan for the Development of a Curative Institute in the South of Ireland sent in 1938 by Dr König to the Irish Government

Since that period of cultural development of man when he started to settle in communal settlements it occurred time and again that human beings were born who stood out through certain abnormal features. (Such abnormalities do not belong into the realm of illness, since illness is of a passing nature). These abnormities manifested themselves in the fact that those afflicted by them were unable to be part of a normal group of settlers. It was therefore customary that the settlement concerned would take on joint responsibility for these abnormal people.

A long as man was a hunter, as long as his settlements were of a temporary nature it was customary to destroy these abnormal human beings. When, however, the hunter developed into a farmer and tiller of the earth, that means that his communal settlement became of a fixed nature, linked to the soil, these abnormal people were cared for. Today still the village cares for its epileptic or its idiot; it provides him with suitable work, looks after him and feeds him.

With the development of the big cities the measure of the abnormal people increased too, so that the number of those who could not be incorporated into .town and city communities grew ever larger. Public and private welfare institutions took on these people and tried to do their best for them.

For this reason the large asylums were built which took up the task to facilitate for the abnormal an existence worthy of a human being. Furthermore there arose special schools which tried to lead abnormal children so far in their development that they would reach a level of normality which would allow to integrate them into the family and society at large.

It showed however more and more that only a small part of these children are so far educable and malleable that, being left to their own devices, they can lead an independent life. These children having become adults find it rather difficult to take up an ordinary profession and to hold their own ground in the vicissitudes of daily existence. The result is that they are put into asylums in common with the disabled old person or with the so called incurable patient and there they are to wait tardily for a miserable death.

...He, however, who has lived, as I did, for many years with such children and adults, he who knows them and has learned to perceive their peculiarities, abilities and human faculties, can arrive more and more at the conviction that a depository is not a suitable solution for them but that every one of these human beings - put in the right place - can prove himself and find his niche. These abnormal children and adults are not ill patients but-such that have lost their path. A world that thinks and feels in a Christian way must give a place to these too. To these people the word of Christ is related which he spoke to his disciples when they asked him if the man born blind was a sinner, saying that "it was not that this man sinned or his parents but that the works of God might be manifest in him" (John 9, 3).

Such are these abnormal people: they have come into the world in order that the works of God may become manifest in them and they wait that people be found who would help them to lead a life that is justified and worth living. What has been done so far in human society for the blind should be extended to all the abnormal people. It should be extended to those who are blind in their thinking or their willing, who are slow or lame, to the epileptic and the shaking, to the deaf and the dumb. They all deserve that they would find a community in which they would be able to live and to take up the tasks and the work which is within their abilities.

This work shall, however, not be constituted in such a way that this would disadvantage the one who stands in the normal process of work, i.e. that the production of these abnormal people would harm any other production by way of competition. The aim should be that these children and adults would be united under the guidance of those who put themselves at their disposal into a self-sufficient place which can become a community answering the needs of these people. For all those who are expelled from human society (excluding criminals, thieves etc. - corrective institutions are available for these and the realm of jurisdiction is responsible for them) a working community under the auspices of the Department of Educational Medicine and Social Services of the concerned country should be created wherein they could be self-supporting to a larger or lesser degree. If one would take the mark of inferiority from the foreheads of these children they will show their hidden potential. They are inferior only within ordinary society but not within their own context. In that context they complement one another like the blind and lame and they form in their togetherness a whole and fully adequate community. Such a community is able to be self-supporting. It will thereby relieve the state of a burden and will provide for those working in it a worthy existence.

The necessary foundation of such a community is a purposefully led farm. This farm would have to include all earth-tilling activities. One would have to grow both corn for bread baking and animal fodder. There would have to be enough milking cows to supply the community with milk and to provide a butter and cheese making dairy with its surplus. A large garden would have to supply the most necessary vegetables and the most common fruit and berries. Linked with it should be a chicken farm, a piggery and some sheep breeding which would cover the needs of the community. All this should, however, be started in a small fashion and should be gradually increased following the growth of the community. What is lost through the lack of ability in the work force - for this should consist mainly, with the exception of the workmasters, of the residents - must be made up by well-planned and intensive farming. Experience has shown that every abnormal human being can learn and execute some work-process if it is limited in time and complexity, e.g. milking only or handling cattle only, or sowing only. The process thus learned will be repeated with an unshakeable steadiness and firmness.

The farm in turn demands the development of some workshops which are also to be run by the abnormal residents. A basic cartwright's and wheelright's shop, a -joinery, a locksmith's shop and a simple forge. Also these fundamental and simple work processes can be learned by retarded people. It would however be dangerous and irrational if these workshops would accept outside orders since any intensified production that would enter into competition with others is beyond the scope of such workshops. Only the immediate needs of the whole settlement are a suitable target for the production of these workshops.

In this way the work on the land is the foundation of this settlement; linked to it are the workshops which shall not only be production workshops but also training workshops since those who work there get their new reinforcements from the centre of the settlement - that is the institute for curative education. First a few details about the`" structure of this institute. It shall at first cater only 'for children. These retarded children are not only to be kept in this home but first and foremost they shall be educated. A home school with its teacher will care for the education of these children. Since. it should follow the policy of admitting any child in need it should not have a fixed fee but one that is linked to the income of the parents or relatives who place the child. Even the state or the local authorities should be allowed to place poorer or poorest children for smaller contributions. The fee paid, however, is to have no influence on the care and education of the child. All children should be catered for in the same way. Those who place the child provide clothing and bedding (In special cases some exceptions can be made since some needy children could be supplied by clothes which have become too small).

The institute cares for the mending and care of clothes. This provides an opening for a small tailor's and cobbler's workshop.

The laundry is washed in a laundry that is run and manned by the members of the settlement.

Dr König enters then into some questions of finance, envisages one or two central kitchens for the provision of meals and linked to them a bakery and a butcher's shop. He describes that the female residents should work as household helpers and in the garden. He says that "the centre of the institute should be a school" and describes the way of education and the emphasis on art. He also discusses the care which should be given to the severely subnormal and describes the position of the medical doctor in the settlement. The tasks and the rights of the staff are then detailed, as well as the administration of the place and its financial running.

Dr König ends his essay with the following considerations: The Christian faith is to be the religious foundation of the settlement. It shall, however, not have the form of a denominational doctrine but of a free creed. Specific personalities nominated by the council of elders shall hold devotions for all residents on Sundays and on festivals. Religion lessons are to be given by teachers designated by the small conference of teachers.

It shall, however, be open to every child to be educated in the religious creed wished for or stipulated by the parents, provided that it is a Christian one.

The daily routine of the home shall be strictly ordered. It begins and ends with a short devotion. The meals are common as far as possible. The work on the farm and in the workshop must, however, not be disrupted thereby.

Common sitting rooms, a library, a hall with a stage and other cultural provisions shall be gradually. developed. The coworkers who wish to join the work permanently are to develop an inner striving which equips them every day and hour for their task. They give to one another common theoretical and practical lessons in order to further their advance. The true meaning of such a venture can only consist in serving the striving human being that he become an ever stronger Christian through sacrifice and surrender and that he receive healing by being a healer.

The complete planning of the venture proposed here is the result of nine years experience, first as assistant in a similar home in Switzerland for one year, then as leader of such an institute in Silesia through eight years.

In this plan are gathered and sifted all the good and bad experience-of those years and I trust that the execution of it is entirely possible and assure if but a beginning can be made.

Such an institution would be unique today and would be a credit to the country in which it would be developed.

Notes

HMW is Hans Müller-Wiedemann, *Karl König, a Central European Biography of the Twentieth Century.*

Foreword

1. Steiner, *Wahrspruchworte,* p. 97.
2. Peter Selg, *Anfänge anthroposophischer Heilkunst.*

Autobiogaphical Fragment

1. Steiner, *Geistige Wirkenskräft,* p.186.
2. Steiner, *Geistige Wirkenskräft,* p.191.

A Biographical Sketch

1. Letter of Oct 13, 1902 to Wilhelm Hübbe-Schleiden, in Steiner, *Briefe,* Vol. 2, p. 309.
2. Autobiographical Fragment, see p. 17.
3. Autobiographical Fragment, see p. 17.
4. Bertha König, *Memoirs,* p. 56.
5. Bertha König, *Memoirs,* p. 62.
6. Autobiographical Fragment, see p. 18
7. Autobiographical Fragment, see p. 18
8. HMW, p. 26.
9. Selg, 'Eine kurze Skizze der Geschichte anthroposophischer Medizin bis zum Tode Rudolf Steienrs,' in Selg, *Anthroposophische Ärzte,* p.36
10. HMW, p. 32.
11. Autobiographical Fragment, see p. 18.
12. Autobiographical Fragment, see p. 21.
13. Autobiographical Fragment, see p. 19.

14. Autobiographical Fragment, see p. 19.
15. Autobiographical Fragment, see p. 19.
16. HMW, p. 41.
17. Steiner, *Briefe,* Vol. 1, p. 13.
18. Autobiographical Fragment, see pp. 19f.
19. Letter of Nov 4, 1894 to Rosa Mayreder. *Briefe,* Vol. 2, p. 232.
20. Autobiographical Fragment, see pp. 20f.
21. Autobiographical Fragment, see p. 21.
22. Autobiographical Fragment, see p. 25.
23. Autobiographical Fragment, see p. 22.
24. Autobiographical Fragment, see p. 23.
25. Kurt Magerstädt, 'Einer von den Jungmedizinern,' in M.J. Krück von Poturzyn, *Wir erlebten Rudolf Steiner,* p. 141.
26. König, 'The Candle on the Hill,' in HMW, p. 65.
27. HMW, p. 65.
28. Autobiographical Fragment, see pp. 27f.
29. Autobiographical Fragment, see p. 28.
30. Selg, *Ita Wegman und Karl König,* p. 223.
31. Selg, *Ita Wegman und Karl König,* p. 223.
32. König, *Vom Wirken des Arztes,* p. 256.
33. Unpublished manuscript in HMW, p. 97.
34. Autobiographical Fragment, see p. 34.
35. HMW, p. 98.
36. Selg, *Ita Wegman und Karl König,* pp. 110f.
37. Selg, *Ita Wegman und Karl König,* p. 125.
38. Autobiographical Fragment, see p. 36.
39. Compare the Erich Kirchner's letter of June 20, 1933 to Ita Wegman, in Selg, *Geistiger Widerstand und Überwindung,* p.33.
40. Selg, *Ita Wegman und Karl König,* pp. 57f.
41. Unpublished manuscript, in HMW, p. 105.
42. Autobiographical Fragment, see p. 40.
43. 'Life with Dr König,' see p. 136.
44. König, *Vom Wirken des Arztes,* p. 256.
45. Autobiographical Fragment, see p. 41.
46. Rath, 'Von der Begegnung der Jugend,' in Belte and Vierl, *Erinnerungen,* p. 397.
47. Rath, 'Von der Begegnung der Jugend,' in Belte and Vierl, *Erinnerungen,* p. 398.
48. Peter Roth, 'Vor dem zweiten Weltkrieg in Wien,' unpublished manuscript, quoted in HMW, pp. 112f.
49. HMW, p. 125.
50. HMW, p. 444.
51. HMW, p. 445f.
52. Steiner, *Geistige Wirkenskräfte,* p.197.

53. König, 'Die drei Leitsterne der Camphill-Bewegung,' pp. 7f.
54. König, 'Die drei Leitsterne der Camphill-Bewegung,' pp. 9f.
55. Unpublished manuscript, quoted in HMW, p. 149.
56. Anke Weihs, 'Fragments from the Story of Camphill,' quoted in HMW, p. 149.
57. HMW, p. 449.
58. HMW, pp. 153f.
59. 'Zwischen Dee und Bodensee,' unpublished manuscript, quoted in HMW, p. 158.
60. König, 'Die drei Leitsterne der Camphill-Bewegung,' p. 12.
61. 'Zwischen Dee und Bodensee,' unpublished manuscript, quoted in HMW, p. 158.
62. HMW, p. 140.
63. HMW, p. 161.
64. From a talk of August 30, 1953, quoted in HMW, p. 456.
65. Selg, *Ita Wegman und Karl König,* pp. 235f.
66. Selg, *Ita Wegman und Karl König,* p. 237.
67. Heidenreich, 'Dr Karl König,' *Christian Community Journal,* 1966. p. 129.
68. HMW, p. 196.
69. HMW, p. 207.
70. König, *Der Kreis der zwölf Sinne,* p.109.
71. Selg, *Ita Wegman und Karl König,* p. 88.
72. König, *Auch eine Weihnachtsgeschichte,* p. 35.
73. HMW, p. 181.
74. König, 'Die drei Leitsterne der Camphill-Bewegung,' p. 38.
75. HMW, p. 245.
76. HMW, p. 248.
77. Letter of Feb 10, 1951 to Carlo Pietzner, quoted in HMW, p. 251.
78. Diary entry of Jan 22, 1945, quoted in HMW, p. 254.
80. HMW, p. 317.
81. HMW, p. 283f.
82. HMW, p. 270f.
83. HMW, p. 271.
84. König, 'In Memory of a Friend.'
85. HMW, p. 271–73.
86. HMW, p. 285.
87. HMW, p. 290.
88. Letter of Nov 6, 1959 to Hans Müller-Wiedemann, in HMW, p. 333. This comment should be seen in the light of the 'Kirkton House Address' given by Dr Karl König on May 28, 1939:

    It is significant that we are here in Scotland, where the great Hibernian Mysteries were active which, although they were of pagan origin, received Christianity and contributed towards the Christianizing of Great Britain.

Rudolf Steiner spoke of two streams of Christianity. One stream, which came from the East associated with forces of the blood, began with the Disciples and spread westwards as the Grail stream of Christ. The second stream, which originated in Ireland, Scotland and Cornwall, crossed to the Continent and united with the other stream in Central Europe.

As a spiritual prelude of these developments the Council of Constantinople took place in AD 869, an event which had great significance for the human soul, for it was there that the decision was taken to abolish the spirit and to conceive of man as consisting only of body and soul, together with certain spiritual faculties which live in the soul.

If one travels through the countryside here, one can have the impression that Christianity must be brought back and that this is possible in a transformed way through anthroposophy.

We must understand this rightly. It is not that we should see ourselves as the bearers of a mission, but that we should try to bring about a meeting between the English spirit and the spirit of Central Europe, a meeting between everything that has been dreamt and thought by the German spirit and that which the English spirit can accomplish by way of deeds. We should promise one another not to create an island of Central Europe here but to try as well as we can to act for the good of this land. We want to try to achieve this in the knowledge that even if we fail, others will succeed. But let us try and perhaps the spirit will allow us to make such a contribution.

(There followed a reading by Karl König of the *Foundation Stone Meditation.)*.

89. HMW, p. 335.
90. HMW, p. 337.
91. HMW, p. 334.
92. König, 'American Impressions,' also quoted in HMW, p. 341.
93. König, 'Amerika, hast du es besser?' p. 9.
94. HMW, pp. 365f.
95. HMW, p. 407.
96. HMW, p. 407.
97. HMW, p. 410.
98. HMW, p. 436.
99. HMW, p. 542
100. HMW, p. 407.
101. HMW, p. 414.

Bibliography

Beltle, Erika and Vierl, Kurt (Eds.), *Erinnerungen an Rudolf Steiner,* Stuttgart 1979.

König, Bertha, *Memoirs of Childhood and Life,* unpublished manuscript, n.d. (Karl König Archive).

König, Karl, 'American Impressions,' in *The Cresset,* Vol. VI, No. 5, Michaelmas 1960 and Vol. II, No. 2, Christmas 1960.

—, 'Amerika, hast du es besser?' in *Die Kommenden,* Vol. 17, No. 1.

—, *Auch eine Weihnachtsgeschichte,* Stuttgart 1998.

—, 'Die drei Leitsterne der Camphill-Bewegung,' in Alix Roth (Ed.), *Die Camphill-Bewegung,* Brachenreuthe 1965.

—, 'In Memory of a Friend.' *Beiträge zu einer Erweiterung der Heilkunst nach geisteswissenschaftlichen Erkentnissen,* Nos. 11/12, 1953.

—, *Der Kreis der zwölf Sinne und die sieben Lebensprozesse,* Stuttgart 1999.

—, 'Vom Wirken des Arztes in der heutigen Zeit,' unpublished manuscript.

Krück von Poturzyn, M.J. (Ed.), *Wir erlebten Rudolf Steiner. Erinnerungen seiner Schüler,* Stuttgart 1967.

Lehrs, Ernst, 'Wie es zum "Pädogogischen Jugendkurs" kam' (How the Youth Course came about), in *Mitteilungen aus der Anthroposophischen Gesellschaft in Deutschland,* Easter 1956.

Müller-Wiedermann, Hans, *Karl König, A Central European Biography of the Twentieth Century,* Camphill Press 1996.

Rath, Wilhelm, 'Von der Begegnung der Jugend mit Rudolf Steiner auf dem "Pädogogischen Jugendkurs" Michaeli 1922' (From the meeting of Rudolf Steiner with the young people at the Youth Course at Michaelmas 1922) in Belte and Vierl, *Erinnerungen,* p. 397.

Roth, Alix (Ed.), *Die Camphill-Bewegung,* Brachenreuthe 1965.

Selg, Peter, *Anfänge anthroposophischer Heilkunst,* Dornach 2000.

—, *Anthroposophische Ärzte. Lebens- und Arbeitswege im 20. Jahrhundert,* Dornach 2000.

—, *Geistiger Widerstand und Überwindung. Ita Wegman 1933–1935,* Dornach 2005.

—, *Ita Wegman und Karl König. Eine biographische Dokumentation,* Dornach 2007 (English: *Ita Wegman and Karl König. Letters and Documents,* Edinburgh 2008).
—, *Karl König's Path into Anthroposophy,* Edinburgh 2008.
Steiner, Rudolf, *Briefe,* Vol. 1, Complete Works (GA) 38, Dornach 1985.
—, *Briefe,* Vol. 2, GA 39, Dornach 1987.
—, *Helipädagogischer Kurs,* GA 317, Dornach 1985. English: *Education for Special Needs* (Curative Education Course), Forest Row 2005.
—, *Geistige Wirkenskräfte im Zusammenleben von alter und junger Generation. Pädogogischer Jugendkurs.* GA 217. Dornach 1964. English: *Becoming the Archangel Michael's Companions: Rudolf Steiner's Challenge to the Younger Generation,* Massachussets 2007.
—, *Die Philosophie der Freiheit,* GA 4, Dornach. English: *Philosophy of Freedom,* Forest Row 1999, or *Intuitive Thinking as a Spiritual Path,* New York 1995.

Index

Aberdeen 12, 14, 91
Advent garden 28, 71, 72
Advent garden experience 121
America 123
Andrian, Baron 50
Anthroposophical Society 74, 94, 107f, 120f
Arlesheim 69
Arnim, Georg and Erika von 131
Austrian annexation 1938 44, 84, 89

Beethoven, Ludwig von 148
Bennachie (dream about) 95
Bobath, Mrs (movement therapist) 113
Bock, Emil (priest of the Christian Community) 79f
Brachenreuthe 127

Calvin, Johann 15
Camphill (estate) 15f, 102f
Catholic Curch (Karl's baptism) 58
Chamberlain, Neville (prime minister) 51
Christian Community, the 107
Clinical Therapeutic Institute, Arlesheim 25, 69
Colchis Mysteries 88
Collot d'Herbois, Liane 125
Curative Education Course (Steiner's) 26, 30, 98
Cyprus, appeal to 47, 89

Daladier, Edouard (French president) 51
Darwin, Charles 101
Dunlop, Daniel Nicol (chairman of Anthroposophical Society in GB) 35, 77, 125

East-West Congress, 1922 21, 86
Emmichoven, W Zeylmans van *see* Zeylmans van Emmichoven, Dr Frederik Willem
Engel, Dr Hans-Heinrich (Camphill co-worker) 8, 150
Engel, Margit (Camphill co-worker) 130

Fischel, Prof Alfred (director of Institute of Embryology) 21, 25
Francis of Assisi 88
Franz Joseph, Emperor 17

Glas, Norbert and Maria 66
Glencraig 157
Gnadenfrei 31f
Goethe, Johann Wolfgang von 18, 50, 60

Haeckel, Ernst 25, 30, 66
Hahnemann, Samuel Friedrich (founder of homeopathy) 23
Hardt, Dr Heinrich 30
Hauser, Kaspar 109, 156

Heathcot 105
Heidenreich, Alfred (priest of the Christian Community) 107
Herbois, Liane Collot d' *see* Collot d'Herbois, Liane
Hermanus (South Africa) 123
Herrnhuter brotherhood 32, 75, 102
Heydebrandt, Caroline von (Waldorf teacher) 35
Hitler, Adolf 44, 84, 89
Hohenfurth Monastry, Moravia 43, 88
homeopathy 23, 62
Huberman, Bronislav (violinist) 51
Hume, David (philosopher) 14

Institute of Embryology, Vienna 21, 25, 60, 66
Irish Republic, appeal to 47, 89

Jeetze, Joachim and Dorothea von (owner of Pilgrimshain) 34

Karlstein Castle 127
Kirkton House 95
Klosterneuburg 23, 67
Knox, John 15
Kolisko, Dr Eugen 20, 35, 64, 66, 68, 77, 92, 94f, 99f, 118, 125
König, Adolf (Karl's father) 55f
König, Bertha (Karl's mother) 55f
König, Tilla (née Mathilde Elisabeth Maasberg) 30–32, 35f, 46, 49, 70, 74–76, 79, 88, 95, 98, 103

Lauenstein (institute) 26, 30
Lemmermeyer, Fritz 35
Löffler, Franz 30
London 35, 77

Maasberg, Lena (Tilla König's sister) 31f, 75
Maasberg, Maria (Tilla König's sister) 30, 32, 70
Maasberg, Tilla *see* König, Tilla
Macleod, Georg 105
Magerstädt, Dr Kurt (physician) 67
Mahler, Gustav 148, 156
Man, Isle of 102f, 105
Marco, Donna Lucia de Viti de 49
Marti, Dr Ernst 51
Maryculter 16
Meyer, Rudolf (priest of the Christian Community) 147
Molay, Jakob von (last Grand Master of the Knights Templar) 17, 46
Müller, Hans (writer) 50
Müller-Wiedemann, Hans 8, 111, 115, 117, 126

Oberufer Nativity play 41, 86, 93
Ostmark, spiritual 83

Paris 51, 90
Pedagogical Youth Course (Steiner's) 42, 44, 86–88
Philippe the Fair 17
Pilgrimshain 34, 36, 76–80, 82f

Reid, Thomas (philosopher) 14
Rittelmeyer, Friedrich (priest of the Christian Community) 35, 77
Rosenkreutz, Christian 98
Roth, Alix (one of founders of Camphill) 95, 153
Roth, Peter (one of founders of Camphill) 87, 105
Roux, Wilhelm (anatomist) 21

Schickler, Dr Eberhard (physician) 35, 119, 123
Schröer, Karl Julius 86
Schubert, Dr Karl (Waldorf teacher) 35, 77
Sonnenhof (institute) 27, 70
South Africa 120f
Stein, Dr Walter Johannes 35, 56
Steiner, Rudolf 19–22, 26, 63f, 66f, 74, 86, 101, 111, 121

Stifter, Adalbert (Austrian writer) 43, 88
Stöhr, Prof Adolf 18
Storm, Theodor (poet) 12
Strohschein, Albrecht 30, 32f, 70, 75

Templar, Knights 16f
Teschner, Richard (artist) 19

United States of America 123

Vienna 17f, 21–23, 36f, 40, 84
Vienna, University of 18, 59

Wegman, Ita 25–29, 34f, 50f, 68f, 72–74, 77f, 90f, 108f, 118, 125
Weihs, Anke (one of founders of Camphill) 8, 85, 96, 132
Weihs, Dr Thomas (one of founders of Camphill) 95, 157
Williamstown 92

Zeylmans van Emmichoven, Dr Frederik Willem 34, 76, 122f, 125
Zinzendorf, Count 32, 102, 117
Zuckmayer, Carl (playwright) 50
Zwätzen (institute) 30

Karl König's collected works are being published in English by Floris Books, Edinburgh and in German by Verlag Freies Geistesleben, Stuttgart. They are issued by the Karl König Archive, Aberdeen in co-operation with the Ita Wegman Institute for Basic Research into Anthroposophy, Arlesheim. They seek to encompass the entire, wide-ranging literary estate of Karl König, including his books, essays, manuscripts, lectures, diaries, notebooks, his extensive correspondence and his artistic works. The publications will fall into twelve subjects.

The aim is to open up König's work in a systematic way and make it accessible. This work is supported by many people in different countries.

Overview of Karl König Archive subjects

Medicine and study of the human being
Curative education and social therapy
Psychology and education
Agriculture and science
Social questions
The Camphill movement
Christianity and the festivals
Anthroposophy
Spiritual development
History and biographies
Artistic and literary works
Karl König's biography

Karl König Archive
Camphill House
Milltimber
Aberdeen AB13 0AN
United Kingdom
www.karl-koenig-archive.net
kk.archive@camphill.net

Ita Wegman Institute for Basic Research into Anthroposophy
Pfeffingerweg 1a
4144 Arlesheim
Switzerland
www.wegmaninstitut.ch
koenigarchiv@wegmaninstitut.ch